Church On Fire!

a testimony of revival

as told by Pastor Morris Vaagenes

Morris G. O. Vaagenes

Renewal International
3540 Harriet Avenue • Shoreview, MN 55126

CHURCH ON FIRE
a testimony of revival

PASTOR MORRIS VAAGENES

Copyright © 2008 by Morris Vaagenes

ISBN 978-1-60702-324-1
Published by Renewal International
3540 Harriet Avenue, St. Paul, MN 55126

Acknowledgements

I wish to thank my wife Bonnie, who has been a valuable partner with me in ministry. She has been my strongest supporter, my closest friend, and best critic through the past half century. When I was downcast, I could share the situation with her, and she would lift me up. When I was going in a wrong direction, she became my course-corrector.

Our children, Lois, Paul, Timothy, and Mark, were active participants and supporters also, as well as the ones who would bring me down to earth if I was acting too exalted. The sacrifices made by my family were significant and often unnoticed. They, together with all the wonderful people of God who were part of this ministry, made North Heights an exciting place to serve. They are the real North Heights story.

I record North Heights' venture of faith from my personal experience and viewpoint. A dozen years ago I met Lyle Schaller, a leading church consultant and author, at the Crystal Cathedral in Garden Grove, California where we were both speakers at an institute on church leadership. He encouraged me to write this account, weaving together the North Heights story with my own autobiography as concurrent story lines. I am following his advice, and thus this book.

I wish to honor the numerous faithful people through whom the Lord has done the work I have written about in this book. To name all the dedicated ministers of the Lord who devoted themselves, their time, their labors, and their resources to this endeavor would be an impossible undertaking. Thus, while only a few heroes of faith are identified, the omission of the many other devoted servants of the Lord should not diminish their valuable contributions. The Lord keeps perfect record in heaven and will reward each one from His vantage point. While all glory belongs to God, deep gratitude belongs to all who served and sacrificed to make this great work possible.

Table of Contents

Church On Fire

The Holy Spirit And With Fire
Introduction

*". . . He will baptize you with the Holy Spirit
and with fire." (Matthew 3:11)*

*"I came to cast fire upon the earth; and would that
it were already kindled!" (Luke 12:49)*

The story is told of a picturesque white frame church situated in the countryside on a high point visible for miles. One evening just after dusk this landmark church caught fire, and the blazing building attracted quite a crowd of spectators.

Not far away lived a local farmer who considered himself quite a skeptic, and who often boasted that he had never darkened the door of a church. But on seeing the building ablaze he hurried to the scene, where a neighbor approached him and commented jokingly, "It's strange seeing you here. What brings you to church?"

To which the farmer responded with a wry, sly smile, "This is the first time I have seen this church on fire."

Can the Church Be Revived?

There may be some telling truth in the skeptic's quick-witted quip. Why are not more people attracted to church? May it be that they see in it too little fire and fervency? A Catholic priest aptly expressed to me the problem, "The church is geared for the lukewarm." No wonder it is not on fire. A church that is hot—and not cold or lukewarm—will have fantastic drawing power.

i

Church On Fire

As I grew up, the daily prayer I heard from my parents was for revival, and their request has become my lifelong quest: for God's mighty manifest presence to be among His people and for the church to express Christ's incarnate life, love, compassion, power, and unity to the world. From my youth, I have been propelled by the dream of the church coming alive spiritually, and consequently growing significantly. My heart's-cry for North Heights to become a spiritually awakened church seemed to me a nearly impossible request when I began to pray it in 1962.

"Can the church be revived?" I asked myself. It appeared to me that dynamic churches existed in other places and at other times, but not where I found myself. Somehow it seemed that revivals took place long ago or far away. How I longed for revival and the Spirit-filled life to be birthed within me and my church!

When I was fifteen, I put to memory Jesus' astounding declaration, recorded in John 14:12:

> "Truly, truly, I say to you, he who believes in me will
> also do the works that I do; and greater works than these
> will he do, because I go to the Father."

How I longed to see this promise fulfilled!

In my short stint as a missionary and in my first pastorate, I found that human effort and zeal can, indeed, raise the level of life and activity in a congregation, but not to the level that Jesus had promised. What was wrong? What was missing? Can a church come alive spiritually? These were questions that consumed me.

A Prophetic Promise of Restoration

I noted in my biblical studies that repentance and the restoration of God's chosen people were the message and mission of the Old Testament prophets. But too frequently their warnings and invitations were rejected. Yet even during Israel's most apostate times, God gave His messengers visions of restoration. They proclaimed this message of hope into hopeless settings.

Ezekiel's vision of the valley of dry bones (chapter 37:1-14) offers a striking picture of revival. Israel is portrayed as dead, dry bones filling a desolate valley. The Lord asks Ezekiel if the bones could live again, to which the prophet answers, "O Lord God, thou knowest."

Then the Lord directs Ezekiel to prophesy, "O dry bones, hear the word of the Lord." The message is that the Lord God would will breath to enter them, they will live, and they will know that He is the Lord. As the prophet speaks the word of the Lord to the bones, they come together, and then tendons, flesh, and skin cover them. But there is no breath in them.

Then the Lord tells Ezekiel to prophesy to the breath (in the Hebrew, wind or spirit) to "breathe upon these slain, that they may live." As he does this, breath comes into them, and they come to life and stand on their feet—"an exceedingly great host" (v.10).

The Lord explains to Ezekiel that the vision is a picture of Israel during the darkest period in her history. Due to her grave spiritual and moral depravity, God allowed Israel to be conquered by Babylon, her cities and temple utterly destroyed, and the bulk of the nation deported from the "promised land" to a far-off country. There appeared no hope for reconciliation with God or for restoration to her homeland. But God's message to His people through Ezekiel is to assure them that He will revive them.

Two directives were given to the prophet, as already noted. First, he was to speak the Lord's life-giving prophetic word to moribund Israel. This was not to be a message of condemnation, but of consolation. The second command was that Ezekiel petition the Spirit to breathe His breath of life into them so that they could live. As Ezekiel spoke the word of the Lord to the bones and to the Spirit, the people came alive.

The vision given to Ezekiel is an encouraging message to the church now, as it has been at every point in its history—that there is hope for renewal, and that the Lord is in the reviving business. In Ezekiel's vision, Israel confesses her helplessness and hopelessness, and she recognizes her desperate condition. This is a good starting point for revitalization, to lament the current dead condition and to acknowledge the cause, i.e., spiritual apathy.

North Heights Renewal

This book is the story of how a pastoral couple, Bonnie and I, together with a congregation, North Heights Lutheran Church in suburban St. Paul and Minneapolis, Minnesota, experienced exciting spiritual renewal over a period of several decades. It is my own spiritual journey that helped shape my ministry. Central in my life has been the quest for the presence and power of the Holy Spirit so as to enable me to live a victorious Christian life and to minister effectively with abundant fruit for the Kingdom of God.

This is an account of the Holy Spirit's work of transforming lives at North Heights, the body of believers I shepherded for more than thirty-eight years. This book will recount both my and the church's story, and it will include the applied principles that made it a spiritually live, dynamic and effective church.

This account of North Heights Lutheran Church is intended not as our history, but as *His Story*. It is a remarkable story of the Lord choosing ordinary people to do extraordinary work under the Spirit's anointing and in obedient faith. It reveals how God can transform human weakness into divine strength.

This story is not meant to show how good or great we are, but to demonstrate God's amazing grace in action, expressed through common, fallible people. It is an adventure of faith born out of our faltering and feebleness. It is an account of God's faithfulness in the face of our frequent faithlessness.

This is more than a recounting of events that transpired and the people who made them happen. It is also an account of who was behind the scene making it happen—that is, the Holy Spirit—and why and how these things took place. It deals with the inner spirit, heart, love, steadfastness, and courage of the congregation. It is the biblical grace/faith message the Spirit wrote in my heart and then into the very fabric of North Heights' being. This is the DNA that has shaped this body of believers over many decades.

The personality of a church comes out of the spiritual life of its leaders and members. As senior pastor of North Heights for nearly forty years, I obviously played a major role in shaping its faith, theology, and culture, as well as its message, ministry, and mission. As shepherd of the flock, the pastor is called to lead the sheep to the green pastures so that they may be spiritually healthy and reproductive. This I sought to do by the grace and help of God.

Church On Fire

Building on the Foundation

My purpose in writing this story is to preserve for future generations the account of the acts of the Holy Spirit in our midst in our time, so that those who follow may continue to build on this solid foundation. My prayer is that we will all grow into the full dimension of life God has destined for His church, so that we may be filled with all the fullness of the Godhead and may fulfill our mission on earth.

My plea is this: if we as individuals and congregations have abandoned the love we had at first, then we need to remember from what we have fallen, repent, and return to the works we did at first, so that the Lord will not remove our lamp stand, as He spoke to the church at Ephesus:

> *"But I have this against you, that you have abandoned*
> *the love you had at first. Remember then from what you have*
> *fallen, repent and do the works you did at first.*
> *If not, I will come to you and remove your lampstand from its*
> *place, unless you repent." (Revelation 2:4-5)*

My petition is that the Holy Spirit will fall upon us again, to purify us and to ignite us with holy fire from the Lord. My prayer is that the Spirit will do now in us what we read in Scripture, when fire fell from heaven on the sacrifices offered at the dedication of the tabernacle (Leviticus 9:24) and at the dedication of the temple (2 Chronicles 7:1), on Elijah's offering at Mount Carmel (1 Kings 18:38) and on those gathered in the Upper Room on the day of Pentecost (Acts 2:1-4).

At the dedication of the tabernacle, instruction was given to keep the fire that came from heaven onto the altar burning continually and to never let it go out (Leviticus 6:13). This was holy fire ignited by the Lord. No manmade fire was to be offered to the Lord on the altar, for this would be unholy or strange fire. Nadab and Abihu, Aaron's two oldest sons, brought their own unholy fire and offered it to the Lord, contrary to the Lord's clear command. Fire came forth from the presence of the Lord and consumed them, and they died (Leviticus 10:1-2).

We need genuine revival fire initiated in heaven, holy fire ignited by the Lord. All efforts to manufacture revival fire will result in unholy fire. All endeavors to create fire by stirring up emotions will produce strange fire. We need the real thing, fire that will burn off dross, cleanse us of our sins, and set us ablaze for the Lord. If the fire that once burned brightly in us is now barely a flicker, then we need to follow Paul's instruction to Timothy:

For this reason I remind you to fan into flame the gift of God,
which is in you through the laying on of my hands.
For God did not give us a spirit of timidity, but a spirit of power,
of love and of self-discipline. (2 Timothy 1:6-7, NIV)

The revival fire that falls from heaven in the outpouring of the Holy Spirit is truly holy fire. Most likely there have been times throughout the years when we individually and collectively have cooled off in our relationship with the Lord, and as a result the embers died down, and we became lukewarm. A coal will lose its warmth rapidly if it separates itself from other burning coals that are in the heat of fire. If that describes your situation, I beg you to repent of your backsliding and return to the Lord, and to the fellowship of the warmhearted, to those on fire for the Lord. Otherwise you may be in grave danger for your soul. We pray, "Lord, revive us again!"

Church On Fire

From the Pulpit to the Pew

If there is no fire in the pulpit, there will be no fire in the pew. If there is no fire in the belly of the pastor, how can you expect fire in the hearts of the parishioners? Pastors, do you have a passion for the Lord? Do you have a burden for the salvation of the lost? Do you earnestly desire a church on fire for the Lord? Remember, the divine fire needs to be kindled in your life first, in order for it to burn in the hearts of your members.

The apostle Paul expressed divine jealousy for the churches he planted, that they would continue to build on the foundation he so carefully laid. I have a similar burden for the church for which I poured out my heart and life. Thus, my objective in this book is to recount the Lord's mighty acts, for this truly has been His doing. As we behold what the Lord has done, may we and all future generations give Him glory, thanks, and praise. The psalmist expressed this sentiment, declaring, "Let this be recorded for a generation to come, so that a people yet unborn may praise the Lord" (Psalm 102:18).

Another reason I have written this divine drama is to spark in your heart a Spirit-inspired vision concerning who you are in Christ and what He desires to do through you as you dream His dreams, see His visions, and obey His voice. The Lord has a unique purpose and plan for you. I pray that in reading this account, visions and dreams with be sparked in your heart.

I pray that you will read this book with the desire to know the Lord Jesus Christ more fully and to experience His blessings more richly. Please read it with the prayer that you might be all the Lord has created and redeemed you to be, and that you might accomplish all that He has called you to do. May you be blest far beyond anything you ever dreamed or imagined possible!

Just as the apostle Paul prayed over the Ephesians, I pray over you,

> . . . that out of [the Father's] glorious riches he may
> strengthen you with power through
> his Spirit in your inner being,
> so that Christ may dwell in your hearts through faith.
> And I pray that you, being rooted and established in love,
> may have power, together with all the saints,
> to grasp how wide and long and high and deep is
> the love of Christ, and to know this love
> that surpasses knowledge – that you may be filled to the measure
> of all the fullness of God.
>
> Now to him who is able to do immeasurably more
> than all we ask or imagine, according to his power
> that is at work within us,
> to him be glory in the church and in Christ Jesus
> throughout all generations, forever and ever!
> Amen. (Ephesians 3:16-21, NIV)

"Come Creator Spirit"
Preface

In 1962, Pope John XXIII opened Vatican II with the prayer, "Come, Creator Spirit," and the Holy Spirit came and breathed fresh life into the Roman Catholic Church. The Catholic Charismatic Renewal movement was a partial answer to his petition.

In the 16th Century John Knox prayed, "Lord, give me Scotland or I die!" The Lord granted his request, and the Church of Scotland experienced a mighty reformation.

In 1962, I began praying a prayer patterned after that of John Knox: "O Lord, give me North Heights, or I die!" This was a plea based on Psalm 2:8: "Ask of me, and I will make the nations your heritage, and the ends of the earth your possession." Many missionaries made this their prayer for the nations they went to serve. Psalm 111:6 indicates the promise for fulfillment of this petition: "He has shown his people the power of his works, in giving them the heritage of the nations." My cry was for spiritual awakening in North Heights Lutheran Church, the congregation where only months earlier I had come to serve. By God's grace He answered my petition.

This book is an account of spiritual transformation wrought by the Holy Spirit in answer to prayer. It is a miracle story. The Lord did it, and to Him alone belongs all the glory.

My prayer is that He will stir your heart to seek Him ever more earnestly and to desire His dynamic working in your life and in your setting to an even greater measure. May He accomplish His life-transforming work in and through you!

Lord Jesus Christ, since this is the exciting story of Your mighty action in human hearts and in Your Church, I ask you to guide me by Your Spirit to write what You want recorded so as to inspire each reader to appropriate all You have won through Your atoning work, to receive the fullness of the Spirit's life and power, and to allow you the freedom to transform into Your image the life, home, and church of each of us.

I pray that You will write your vision for each reader and church on the heart of each one who reads this account so that by the power of the Holy Spirit Your name and glory will be spread over all the earth.

May all glory and honor be to You alone! Amen!"

Faith as a Grain of Mustard Seed
Chapter 1

"For truly, I say to you, if you have faith as a
grain of mustard seed, you will say to this mountain,
'Move from here to there,' and it will move; and nothing
will be impossible to you." (Matthew 17:20)

What an unusual scene! People arriving half an hour early just to be able to find a seat for a church service! The narthex and main hallway to the back of the Parish Education Building packed solid with those waiting for the previous service to be dismissed! How will those in the sanctuary for the previous service get through the waiting throng?

Suddenly the service is over, the doors open, and the crowd exits into the narthex. The convergence of the two groups creates a serious jam. The waiting crowd cannot enter the sanctuary until the previous worshipers are all out. In the meantime the ushers are quickly picking up bulletins and other items left in the pews and folding up chairs in the aisles to allow the next group of worshippers to find seats, only to replace the chairs after all the pews are filled.

As soon as the doors open for the next service, the waiting congregants rapidly fill the auditorium to over-capacity. Chairs are replaced in every aisle and in rows in front of the first pews and behind the last row. When those seats are filled, the rest must stand at the outer perimeters of the sanctuary. Thus the sanctuary is filled to fifty percent above seating capacity. Fortunately the fire marshal is not aware of the over-crowded conditions.

Those who are turned away from the sanctuary hurry to the nearby Fellowship Hall to see if there is any space open there. This service is family oriented with a contemporary flavor. Conditions are similar to that of the sanctuary, with all the seats filled. In fact, those coming late may find that even the standing room on the side and back walls of that large auditorium is already filled up.

So they may walk across the parking lot to the Community Center, the former North Heights Elementary School which the congregation purchased. Services are held in the new gymnasium with fully contemporary style worship music. Again, if worshipers do not arrive well before the service times, they will find this service packed out also.

Drawing People to Jesus

You may ask where such a scene took place Sunday after Sunday, year after year. The church was North Heights Lutheran Church located in Roseville, a northern suburb of St. Paul, Minnesota. The scene described took place from the mid 1970s through the mid 1980s, and into the 1990s a similar scenario took place at the church's two campuses—particularly in regard to the Sunday school.

During that earlier era, seven Sunday morning services were held in three worship locations on North Heights' original twelve-acre campus in Roseville. In addition to the worship services, two Sunday school sessions, youth activities, and adult classes filled every available space in the large school building at the 9:30 a.m. and 11:00 a.m. times.

But Sunday morning was not the only time when such activity was taking place. During the week an average of two thousand individuals were involved in a wide variety of programs and ministries for all age groups. Those driving by the church complex on Rice Street in Roseville may have wondered what was going on there, because they would have noticed a large number of vehicles in the parking lots every day and evening of the week.

Today this same thing is taking place at two large campuses in the northern suburbs of St. Paul and Minneapolis, in the cities of Roseville and Arden Hills. North Heights continues to draw thousands to its eleven weekend worship services and to its numerous activities throughout the week.

North Heights Church could be described as a Holy Spirit-charged magnet that drew people from all over the Twin Cities area and as far away as Wisconsin. The focus of all the relationships and activities was the Lord Jesus Christ. It was in allowing the Spirit to lift up and glorify Jesus that people were attracted—not to the church, but to Jesus Christ Himself.

Church On Fire

Why was North Heights able to attract such a large following? What were the keys to its dynamic life and drawing power? How did this take place? Who made it happen? Were there principles in operation that are transferable to other church settings which could lead to their transformation?

Why North Heights? One possible answer is this: Where the Holy Spirit is welcomed and given His proper place by pastor and parishioners, there He will bring new invigorating spiritual life, and there seeking souls will come for refreshing for their spiritual thirst.

Why have so many come to North Heights over the past sixty-plus years? How did North Heights become a dynamic regional mega-church? Who was responsible? What were the factors that led to its development? Can other churches be transformed into vibrant spiritual forces in Christ's kingdom?

I will seek to unfold the process and principles, and especially those biblical truths that became the most significant elements that shaped the members and congregation into a church on fire. It is the Spirit's work from beginning to end. North Heights, as the Lord intends for every congregation, is Christ's body, in which God has made Christ "head over all things for the church, which is his body, the fullness of him who fills all in all" (Ephesians 1:22-23).

A Seed is Sown

The special day, August 17, 1947, had arrived. It was a beautiful summer Sunday afternoon, almost too nice to be indoors. The place was the District 31 School auditorium on the corner of Rice Street and County Road C in rural Ramsey County, two miles north of the St. Paul, Minnesota city limits. The occasion was the Service of Organization for a new congregation, North Heights Community Lutheran Church.

Pastor David Dale, the organizing pastor, led the service. After two hymns and an adult baptism, he brought a message on the theme, "The Hidden Power of the Kingdom of God." The text was Matthew 13:31, 32:

Another parable he put before them, saying, "The kingdom of heaven is like a grain of mustard seed which a man took and sowed in his field; it is the smallest of all seeds, but when it has grown it is the greatest of shrubs and becomes a tree, so that the birds of the air come and make nests in its branches."

Pastor Dale noted that a seed, small as it may be, has invisible life-generating power within it. As it is sown in the ground, it germinates, establishes roots, produces a shoot, enlarges into a trunk with branches and leaves, and ultimately grows into a large tree with abundant fruit. In this way, from the seeds of its fruit, it reproduces itself.

"The Church of Jesus Christ is like a mustard seed," he declared. "At its inception, it appears so very small and insignificant. And so it is with North Heights Lutheran Church. It is beginning in a very small way."

That day of commencement, sixty-six persons, equally divided between children and adults, were received as charter members. Some were transfers from churches in St. Paul, but most of them had been irregular in attendance at their previous church. Others had no church connection prior to the start of this congregation.

Some of those members came when Mrs. Florence Moore went from door to door, and farm to farm or approached shoppers in the grocery store that she and her husband, Sam, owned in the area, encouraging them to join the new congregation. Twenty-four families signed up for membership. Sam and Florence belonged to a church in St. Paul, but rarely attended. The start of a new church in their own community led them to become active members and leaders in the church. Their story was repeated in the lives of several other charter members. This was truly a fertile mission field.

The Holy Spirit, through His invisible and dynamic power, birthed new life in the rural community and in many hearts. The seed was sown in the rich soil of the North Heights community, as the corner of Rice Street and County Road C was called, and it began to sprout, grow, and eventually produce first fruits. Over the past six decades, the small seed sown in faith and energized by the Holy Spirit's power has resulted in multitudes being drawn to partake of North Heights' abundant fruit and to take refuge in its shaded shelter.

A Sunday School is Born

On that Organization Sunday, Pastor Dale noted that just ten months earlier in the same school building, he, together with two neighborhood women, had given birth to a Sunday school. This was a truly indigenous start.

One of the women, Mrs. Mary (Libby) Gervais, and her husband, Louis, lived near the southeast corner of Rice Street and County Road C. Their daughter and family lived next door, and Libby taught her grandchildren Bible stories. Other neighborhood children came to listen to the stories too. In fact, so many children came that there was no longer enough room in the house. So she taught them in the yard.

Libby felt the need for a more formal Sunday school for the community. Ross and Edna Phillips lived at the northeast corner, and Edna had been seeking a Sunday school nearby for her own children, but found none. Thus, in conversation about this need, Libby and Edna decided to take action. Neither felt equipped to develop and conduct a Sunday school, so they sought assistance from a pastor or church.

The first church they contacted referred them to a Bible college in St. Paul, which surveyed the area and concluded that there were not enough children to start a Sunday school. But that did not daunt the zeal of the two women. Another of Libby's neighbors belonged to Rosetown Lutheran Church, located four miles to the southwest. She offered to contact her pastor, David Dale, to see if he would help with the Sunday school. He agreed even without looking at the area. He had started Rosetown Church on his own initiative, and he had the courage to step out in faith in this new location, also. Edna said that she knew one of the school board members, so she asked him about the availability of the school building for this community venture. The request went to Dr. Emmett Williams, superintendent of schools for rural Ramsey County, who gave an affirmative response.

All arrangements worked out beautifully, and on Sunday, October 6, 1946, the first Sunday school session was held. There was excitement on the part of Libby Gervais, Edna Phillips, and Pastor Dale. But there was apprehension as well. How many children would come? Would there be enough to warrant continuing it? In answer to their prayers, eleven children showed up, along with the two founding women, Pastor and Mrs. Dale, plus three teachers from Rosetown Church.

"Certainly the start of the Sunday School was a small beginning, like that of a tiny mustard seed," expressed Pastor Dale in his Organization Sunday message. "But look at what it has become now just ten months later."

A Mission Guild and Worship Service are Birthed

Another step of faith that Pastor Dale referred to in his message was the founding of a mission guild. Several women had expressed interest in further involvement and spiritual growth, and so Pastor and Mrs. Dale assisted them in organizing a mission guild. This took place at the home of Louis and Libby Gervais, with eleven women attending the founding meeting on the cold wintry night of February 25, 1947.

From our perspective today we can see that this small seed has grown into sixty years of vital ministry by thousands of women at North Heights. What an important role women have played in the life of this congregation!

In his message Pastor Dale may also have alluded to the start of worship services on Sunday, May 4, 1947. This was held in the same school auditorium, with Pastor Dale, fourteen adults, and 30 children in attendance. This too was a humble beginning, he noted.

At the Service of Organization, Pastor Dale called attention to the vital role that women and children played in the formation of this new congregation. It was because of concern for the spiritual nurture of children, and as a result of the initiative taken by women, that North Heights Church came into being.

A Congregation is Organized

It was at the June 24, 1947 meeting of the new North Heights Mission Guild that initial steps were taken to organize a congregation. The Rev. John Quanbeck, director of Home Missions for the Lutheran Free Church, was present and explained the procedures they needed to take for incorporation. Florence Moore, a key person in the founding of the congregation, reported that she had received positive response from twenty-four families interested in the organization of a new church in the community.

Sam and Florence Moore offered property adjacent to their store and service station for the site of the new church. Later, the Home Missions Board realized that this parcel would not be large enough, so the Moores donated the value of the property to the building fund, and another location was sought. Mr. and Mrs. Verney Peterson, who owned the farm just north of the school property, donated a parcel to the church.

It is interesting to note that the first gift to the building fund, for $8.96, came from the Sunday school children. "A little child will lead them," we are told in Scripture.

In summary Pastor Dale noted, "Truly the kingdom of God is like the potent power inside a miniscule mustard seed, which when planted in the ground becomes the largest of shrubs and even a good-sized tree which attracts many to come and make their spiritual nests there. The small seed of faith planted in the North

Heights community by three persons grew into eleven children, and now on Organization Sunday it has multiplied to sixty-six charter members, thirty-three children and thirty-three adults. Truly this is living demonstration of God's power at work."

The Seed Becomes a Fruitful Tree

Over sixty years later, we might wonder if perhaps Pastor Dale may have caught a tiny glimpse into the future growth of that seed, and thus may have spoken prophetically about the multitudes that would be attracted to the church and would establish their spiritual nests there. Whether Pastor Dale saw the future's fruitfulness, God, the Creator of the seed, knew what it would become. This was His divine destiny for North Heights.

What kind of tree is North Heights? Is it a giant redwood or a fruitful apple tree? I prefer the latter. A huge redwood is awesome to behold and draws attention to itself, while a fruit tree is not known for its beauty but for its fruit-producing quality. As Dr. Robert Schuller aptly stated, "Anyone can count the seeds in one apple, but only God can count the apples in one seed."

I believe God made North Heights Church to be an apple tree which continues to bear abundant fruit every year and whose seeds are reproducing living fruit in human hearts in the whole region, as well as in communities all across the face of the world. Only God can count the apples that have come from this one seed.

Roland Wells suggests another tree as our model. Roland grew up at North Heights, and it is where he was baptized and confirmed. Now he serves as senior pastor at St. Paul's Evangelical Lutheran Church near downtown Minneapolis, where he has developed a unique and highly acclaimed urban ministry training program.

Roland suggested that the white oak may best reflect the North Heights congregation. White oak trees are slow growing, produce big sweet acorns, are rot resistant, have thick corky protective bark, and can live for hundreds of years. They establish deep roots for food supply and security from violent storms.

The Revolutionary War battleship *The Constitution* was known as Old Ironsides although it was not made of iron, but of northern white oak. The ship derived its name because when cannon balls hit its sides, they just bounced off. Because of her thick sides of resilient white oak, she was able to absorb the destructive force of the cannon balls, and they did not penetrate or destroy the ship. Iron is not resilient like white oak, and would not have been able to withstand the force of the cannon balls.

In contrast to white oak, the strongest tree in the oak family, stands the poplar and other soft wood trees. The poplar grows ten times faster than white oak, but its lifespan is short. Using a play on words, for which Roland is known, he writes that there is poplar Christianity and there are poplar churches sprouting up all over the place. "Poplar Christianity is full of easy answers, dime store theology and warehouse churches that grow today and are gone tomorrow," explains Roland. "They're splashy, explosive, and sprout like crazy. They're certainly not all bad, but they're more like poplars and willows than oaks. Lots of greenery spring up quickly, but it seems they rot too easily, produce little fruit, and their wood has little strength. When they rot or burn, many are deeply wounded."

He adds, "I believe that when we grow a church, it should be a white oak church. Quality fruit. Deep strength. Rot resistance. It's a lot harder to build a white oak church. It takes commitment of each person. It takes sending a tap root deep into God's Word. It means patience, and taking the time to grow strong together. It means doing things like building consensus, listening to each other, making reaching the world with the Gospel the center of our work."

Which ever tree metaphor we choose, whether the mustard tree where birds flock and make their nests, the apple tree with its fruit from which can grow a limitless number of new fruitful trees, or the white oak in all its strength and grandeur, those who have been touched over the years by North Heights can attest to its long life and fruitful service for the kingdom of our Lord and Savior Jesus Christ.

A Look Ahead

If, on that Organization Sunday, August 17, 1947, the congregation's members could have foreseen the fruit sixty years later from that tiny seed, what would they see? The Sunday school, which originated with three adults and eleven children, has grown into a volunteer staff of 500 who minister to 1,600 children between the ages of two years old and sixth grade. Add to that a confirmation program for grades seven through nine with 450 young people who meet every Wednesday for three years to commit their lives to Christ and to get grounded in their faith.

They would marvel at the church's growth from an original membership of 66 multiplying one hundred fold to 6,676 on August 17, 1997, the church's fiftieth anniversary, with 2,500 additional active non-members. Now eleven years later the total number of parishioners has grown to over 7,000.

They would be amazed to see the church property expanded from the original rented space in the District 31 School to two large campuses, both cramped for space because of the continuing growth of the ministries and programs. They would observe one building and expansion program after another.

The first building program was in 1949, when a basement church building was constructed on the original two-acre donated property adjoining the school. A dozen years later the church would purchase an additional four acres, and after five more building and remodeling programs, the congregation was blessed with a beautiful church complex and parsonage on the original Roseville site. Thirty-five years after the start of the Sunday school, the church purchased its original home, the North Heights Elementary School, with all its subsequent additions and eight acres of buildings and playground.

Even that purchase did not meet the physical needs of the burgeoning congregation. Arrangements had to be made for parking at a shopping center north of the church and for shuttle bus service to the church. Every Sunday morning three services were conducted in the enlarged sanctuary, two in the large Fellowship Hall, and two in the new gymnasium in the school building.

After the large facilities on the twelve-acre Roseville campus became so over-crowded that it could not accommodate any more people, the congregation purchased forty-six acres of choice property at an ideal location in Arden Hills. The large sanctuary seating 1,500, and support facilities with classroom and office space, were constructed at the new Arden Hills campus in 1986.

Before long, both campuses were filled to maximum capacity. Temporary modular units were placed on both sites, but even then classes had to meet in hallways. At times, even funerals and weddings had to be turned away because no space was available. Consequently, in 1996 the congregation conducted a fund drive for ministry expansion and debt retirement. An expansive Family Life Center was constructed at the Arden Hills site to alleviate overcrowding at both campuses and to provide opportunities to reach many more persons for Jesus Christ. But even with 250,000 square feet of buildings on both campuses, there is not adequate space to house the burgeoning ministry of the congregation.

Distinctive, Fruitful Ministries

A concern for bringing children into the Kingdom led to the start of a Sunday school and to the founding of a congregation. Children have played a major role in the life of North Heights from the very beginning. In 1986, forty years after the start of the Sunday school, the NeHi Christian Day Care center was opened to provide a Christ-centered and loving environment for pre-school children. Two years later the North Heights Christian Academy was established to provide a quality education and biblical foundation for children to form them into the image of Jesus, who "increased in wisdom and in stature, and in favor with God and man" (Luke 2:52). The school currently has nearly 250 children enrolled in kindergarten through eighth grade.

North Heights is highly committed to sharing Jesus Christ with the community and world. The music and drama department presents two major music and drama productions, the *Passion Play* and *The Splendor of Christmas*, with a combined 36 performances and with participation by over 800 church members in the cast and support services. These productions have been presented annually since 1988 to a total of more than a half million people.

More than sixty missionaries from North Heights have served overseas. The church provides ministries and services to meet a wide variety of needs to its members and the wider community. For four years in the mid-1980s, a television program brought North Heights' message and ministry to stations in a dozen states, parts of Canada, and over Western Europe. Institutes on Church

Renewal inspired church leaders from many states and from all continents to bring spiritual renewal to their churches. A two-year Bible school trained students from across America and around the world in preparation for service in Christ's Kingdom. These are just a few of the dynamic programs and ministries that have multiplied in these sixty years.

Such is the hidden power of the Kingdom of God and of those who have faith as small as a mustard seed. A grandmother, a mother, and a pastor sowed the first seed. Since then, thousands have been actively nurturing what was sown and in turn have been sowing the seed of God's Word in the hearts of others. Only eternity will reveal the fruit that has come from the seed sown in the start of a Sunday school over sixty years ago.

Kingdom Truths at Work

We can identify several themes of God's grace in the initial chapter of the life of North Heights Lutheran Church, themes that continue throughout its rich history.

One is that *God planted the tiny seed known as North Heights Lutheran Church, and only He knows the power and fruit resident within this seed.* God created the seed, placing His own divine power in it. What is true in a natural seed is a reflection of the truth in the spiritual realm.

First John 1:5 tells us that "God is light and in him is no darkness at all." The writer of Hebrews declares: "By faith we understand that the world was created by the word of God, so that what is seen was made out of things which do not appear" (Hebrews 11:3). As God spoke, the visible was created out of the invisible. Genesis 1:3 records, "And God said, 'Let there be light,' and there was light."

The light spectrum—or electromagnetic light and sound waves—includes bands and frequencies within our ability to hear and see, but also those far beyond the human range of hearing and seeing. These include x-rays, gamma rays, ultra-violet rays, etc. God spoke, "Let there be light" and these came into being. We are surrounded by invisible energy far beyond our realization. God placed this invisible dynamic life and light energy within the seed of every plant and tree.

In like manner, this same life power is present through the indwelling divine presence of the Holy Spirit in the believer and in the church, which is the body of Christ, the fullness of Him who fills all things (Ephesians 1:23). Faith releases this creative supernatural power. Our words spoken in faith have unlimited possibilities.

Jesus declared, "For truly, I say to you, if you have faith as a grain of mustard seed, you will say to this mountain, 'Move from here to there,' and it will move; and nothing will be impossible to you" (Matthew 17:20). Without realizing what was transpiring, the founders of North Heights spoke words of faith and thus released God's miraculous power. The result was that the seed was sown in the ground, and this seed has grown into a large, sturdy, fruitful tree with a global outreach. This creative principle has been in operation throughout the congregation's history as people of faith have spoken God's creative word into seemingly impossible situations.

A second theme we see is that *a seed must die in order to be fruitful.* In announcing His own death, Jesus shared with His disciples this principle of fruitfulness: "Truly, truly, I say to you, unless a grain of wheat falls into the earth and dies, it remains alone; but if it dies, it bears much fruit" (John 12:24). Three people gave of themselves so that children could be brought to Jesus. This self-giving faith resulted in that which we see and participate in today. Little did they realize at the time what would be the ultimate fruit of their acts of faith as they started a Sunday school, a women's mission guild, worship services, and a church. Every act of self-giving, of laying down one's life, of crucifixion for Christ's sake, has produced fruit. If there is no crucifixion, there can be no resurrection. To bear fruit, everything must go the way of the cross. This dying to ourselves for the sake of Christ's Kingdom and of reaching people in need of Him has been an integral part of North Heights' DNA. Sacrifice is part and parcel of the church's life and ministry from its founding.

A third truth found in the North Heights story is that *this is completely the Lord's work.* It is His doing from beginning to end. Our history is "His Story." The founders may or may not have been conscious that it was the Lord who placed in their hearts the urge to initiate this great work. But we can see that it was the Lord who did the work through His chosen human instruments. In

Psalm 127:1, King Solomon declares, "Unless the Lord builds the house, those who build it labor in vain." And the apostle Paul tells us that "neither he who plants nor he who waters is anything, but only God who gives the growth" (1 Corinthians 3:7). How encouraging it is to realize the truth of our Lord's words, "I will build my church" (Matthew 16:18). Since it has been the Lord's work from the very beginning, we can take no credit or praise for what has transpired. He declared, "My glory I will not give to another" (Isaiah 48:11). Thus, all glory and praise belongs to God alone.

A fourth lesson is that *the church built on the foundation of Jesus Christ will stand against all evil forces.* Jesus declared: "I will build my church, and the gates of Hades will not overcome it" (Matthew 16:18, NIV). As storms rage from within and from without, the church built on the rock will not be ravaged, but will stand firm (Matthew 7:24-27). As with churches elsewhere, North Heights has survived numerous storms through the decades, and will continue to stand firm on the rock of Christ Jesus.

A fifth thread we note is that *Jesus loves children and invites them to come to Him.* We are reminded, particularly by those involved in children's ministries, that this congregation was started because of a concern for the spiritual welfare of children. The church began out of a Sunday school. It was the Spirit of Jesus at work in the hearts of the founding mother, grandmother, pastor, and teachers that led to the start of the Sunday school. The Bible passage about Jesus blessing little children is very dear to the heart of North Heights:

People were bringing little children to Jesus to have him touch them, but the disciples rebuked them. When Jesus saw this, he was indignant. He said to them, "Let the little children come to me, and do not hinder them, for the kingdom of God belongs to such as these. I tell you the truth, anyone who will not receive the kingdom of God like a little child will never enter it." And he took the children in his arms, put his hands on them and blessed them. (Mark 10:13-16)

A sixth theme is that *the Lord builds his church through ordinary people*. Many may not even have realized that they were channels the Lord was using for building His kingdom. From the very beginning, North Heights has been built by common, ordinary individuals. We note this principle also in Jesus' selection of the twelve apostles to whom He left the commission to build His church: "As he walked by the Sea of Galilee, he saw two brothers, Simon who is called Peter and Andrew his brother, casting a net into the sea; for they were fishermen. And he said to them, 'Follow me, and I will make you fishers of men'" (Matthew 4:18-19).

Later, Jesus makes this declaration to Peter: "And I tell you, you are Peter [in the Greek, *Petros*], and on this rock [in the Greek, *petra*] I will build my church, and the powers of death shall not prevail against it" (Matthew 16:18).

Paul underscores this truth:

For consider your call, brethren; not many of you were wise according to worldly standards, not many were powerful, not many were of noble birth; but God chose what is foolish in the world to shame the wise, God chose what is weak in the world to shame the strong, God chose what is low and despised in the world, even things that are not, to bring to nothing things that are, so that no human being might boast in the presence of God. He is the source of your life in Christ Jesus, whom God made our wisdom, our righteousness and sanctification and redemption; therefore, as it is written, "Let him who boasts, boast of the Lord." (1 Corinthians 1:26-31)

How encouraging this is for each believer! The Lord is building His church all across the globe, and He is choosing willing, humble, obedient persons through whom He does the work. And there is no limit to what He can do through a yielded, obedient person.

The Young Shoot is Watered and Grows
Chapter 2

One planted the seed, another watered it,
but God made it grow. So neither the one who plants
nor the one who waters is anything,
but only God who gives the growth.
The one who plants and the one who waters are equal,
and each will be rewarded according to his labor.
For we are God's fellow workers; you are God's field,
God's building. (1 Corinthians 3:6-9, paraphrased)

Growth was rapid in the church's early years as the farm community was being transformed into suburban housing developments. Pastor Dale served both Rosetown and North Heights churches until late 1948. During the following nine months, Augsburg Seminary students Kenneth Rusdahl and Howard Sortland served on a part-time basis.

A youth ministry, the Luther League, was organized in July of 1949, and the first Vacation Bible School was held that summer. Ellery Severson and Lutheran Bible Institute students assisted in the youth, choir, and Sunday school ministries.

Early Pastoral Leadership and Growth

On August 1949 Pastor Viggo S. Dahle was called as pastor. He served for four years. A basement church was constructed in the fall of 1950 just north of the District 31 School at the cost of

$11,400.00 on land donated by Mr. & Mrs. Verney Peterson. You might call this an "underground church."

A false front was built to provide for a staircase to the basement. This is not the first time a church has put up "a false front." It was the full width of the basement and full height with a cross on top, but it was deep enough only for the staircase. One Sunday noon as people were exiting from the false front at the conclusion of the service, a photographer happened to be driving by on Rice Street. He stopped to observe the large numbers of people coming out of the small false front. I like to tell the story as taking place in the winter with snow covering the basement portion. That isn't exactly the way it was, but it is true that the basement portion was not visible to the photographer. Thus, he was quite amazed to see so many keep coming out of that small building. How could so many fit into such a tiny space? He took a picture and submitted it to the St. Paul newspaper. That was North Heights' first notoriety.

This was Pastor Dahle's last pastorate. He was confined to a wheelchair, but that did not hinder him from visiting all the members and reaching out to new folks who moved into the area. His father was a pastor as well as his three brothers, all serving in the Lutheran Free Church. By 1952, five years after the church's birth, its membership had almost doubled to 121.

Pastor Arthur Kramer was called in 1953 and served for six years. He came into the LFC from the United Lutheran Church in America, a large, more liberal body with German background. Pastor Kramer joined the LFC because of its stance on the authority of the Bible, its emphasis on a personal saving relationship with Christ, and its concern for free and living congregations. He had an effective ministry in leading those outside the Kingdom to conversion and into maturity in their Christian life. One whom he led to the Lord was John (Barney) Oldfield. Barney hung out at the bars after work while at home his wife Grace agonized over his drinking. Pastor Kramer was concerned also and went into the bar to talk with Barney. This resulted in his conversion to faith in Jesus Christ as his Lord and Savior. He became a devoted believer and a strong witness for Christ.

A parsonage was built in 1954 and a sanctuary with office space was constructed above the basement church in 1957 at a cost of $80,000. Much donated labor went into the construction, thus reducing the cost considerably. The first service in the new sanctuary was Christmas Eve in 1957.

Janet Otto began serving as secretary on a volunteer basis in 1955, a position she still holds today, fifty-three years later. Miss Jo Sandvig was called as the church's first parish worker in 1955. She visited 2,000 homes in one year, inviting people to North Heights. Baptized membership grew to 297 by the end of 1958, a 145percent increase during Pastor Kramer's pastorate.

Pastor Calvin J. Storley served two years from 1959 to 1961. Membership increased significantly during his tenure to 525, a 77 percent increase, as housing development in the city of Roseville expanded in the direction of the church.

Pastor Storley visited every home in the congregation each year. His objective was to visit with every member about their relationship with Jesus as Savior and Lord. Miss Ruth Westheim served as parish worker from 1959 to 1962. The growing community continued to be canvassed by Pastor Storley and Miss Westheim, resulting in many new members.

In 1961 an additional four acres behind the church was purchased for $14,000 to prepare for a parish education addition. Contributions increased to the point that Home Mission support was no longer needed.

Each of these early pastors and wives, as well as each member, made significant contributions to the ministry, each with his and her unique gifts and calling. Just as Paul wrote to the Corinthian Church, each laborer in Christ's kingdom contributes to the building of the church.

I count it a privilege to have been chosen of the Lord to be joined with these earlier laborers in the building of this congregation. It is an honor to be a partner in ministry with those who preceded me and to follow in their footsteps. The fruit of their labor lives on after them. And it was a joy to serve with those who labored along side me during my tenure. Each one made a difference in the lives of a multitude of parishioners. And I pray blessings and much fruit from the ministry of those who followed me in this significant endeavor. This is the Lord's temple. He is the head of the church. To Him belongs all glory and honor!

The Lutheran Free Church Foundation

North Heights Lutheran Church was led in its formative years by pastors, seminary students, and parish workers from the Lutheran Free Church (LFC). Among Lutherans of Norwegian heritage the LFC had a distinctive identity. The LFC stamp was imprinted into the very essence of North Heights' personality. Thus, to get a true picture of the church, we need to view from what she was birthed and formed.

The Young Shoot is Watered and Grows

From its inception, North Heights was affiliated with the LFC, a smaller church body with roots stemming from 18th and 19th century spiritual awakenings in Norway known as the Haugean and Johnsonian Awakenings. These revivals had a major impact on the previous pastors, on my life, and in shaping the spiritual life of North Heights and its members.

Hans Nielsen Hauge, a farmer's son, was the anointed instrument for Norway's first major spiritual awakening. On April 5, 1796, he experienced a life-transforming visitation of the Holy Spirit, which gave him new boldness in talking with people about their relationship with the Lord. Bishop Andreas Aarflot, retired Bishop of Oslo in the Lutheran State Church of Norway, ascribed to this experience "the most far-reaching significance." He added, "It is not inconceivable that the April experience had the character of a baptism in the Spirit such as was known later in the Pentecostal movement."

Hauge held fellowship meetings in his home where friends and neighbors came to personal faith in Jesus Christ. Through the Spirit's anointing, his influence spread throughout his region of Norway, and soon he was traveling all across Norway leading thousands to faith in Christ and to awakening in their Christian life. Most, like himself, were lay people.

The spiritual awakening had a strong influence on the social revolution that was taking place in Norway at that time. Starting in the mid 1800s, many of those who experienced awakening through the Hauge movement immigrated to the United States. There they established churches, which continued this emphasis on personal and living faith in Jesus Christ as Savior and Lord.

A second spiritual life movement emerged in Norway in the mid-19th Century and continued for forty years. Gisle Johnson, a theological professor, was the key figure in this awakening. A whole generation of theological students entered into pastoral ministry with the Johnsonian imprint on them. The influence of this renewal was felt strongly among clergy and laity alike.

Rationalism, imported from Germany, swept through the Church of Norway in the 1890s and wiped out much of the impact of the earlier spiritual awakenings. In the early 1900s there was a third awakening that revived the spiritual life from the earlier awakenings. These spiritual awakening movements left a permanent imprint on the religious life of Norway to this day. They produced numerous spiritual life institutions, publications, inner mission societies, foreign mission societies, a free seminary, Bible schools, and prayer houses all across the country.

The revival zeal and spiritual life movements of Norway were carried in the hearts of many immigrants to these American shores. The Lutheran Free Church (LFC), organized in 1897, traced its origin to these pietistic roots. At the time of its founding, many of its congregations were experiencing revival. These spiritual life movements influenced not only the LFC, but other Norwegian Lutheran church bodies in this country as well.

Each of North Heights' earlier pastors came with this pietistic perspective, and it was the foundation on which this congregation was built. I continued that which they had established as the spiritual culture of the church.

I was a speaker at the Centennial Celebration of the Lutheran Free Church in 1997. In preparation for my presentation I re-read our history from several sources. I was amazed to discover how my ministry and that of North Heights were forged and shaped so strongly by our church's founders one hundred years earlier. Some emphases which have been central to my own ministry include:

- The authority of the Word of God for faith and life.
- The necessity for personal salvation through Christ's atoning sacrifice.
- The need for continuous spiritual renewal.
- The significance of free and living congregations.
- The importance of spiritual gifts in the life of a congregation.
- The vital role of laity in witness and mission.
- The importance of evangelistic outreach through world missions.

As I shared my indebtedness to the LFC piety and Fundamental Principles and how they shaped my ministry, I noticed what appeared like jaws dropping and eyes opening wide. Many came to thank me after my presentation. I sensed that some who may have thought I had gone off the deep end by embracing charismatic renewal now realized that I had remained faithful to that on which the LFC was founded.

Guiding Principles

At its founding, the LFC established twelve guiding Fundamental Principles that expressed concern for the spiritual life of its members and congregations. These emphases helped shape my understanding of the Christian faith and of congregational life. They were vital elements in forming North Heights' faith and life. In particular, the following five principles were very influential in my own development, and in the developing ministry of North Heights:

- *According to the Word of God, the congregation (local church) is the right form of the Kingdom of God on earth.*

The Word of God, not the culture or history, sets the standard for what the church should be. For me, the congregation is vital and central in the work of God's Kingdom. As was the heart burden of Georg Sverdrup, the dominant leader in the founding of the LFC and as chief author of the Fundamental Principles, so also my concern has been to build up the local congregation to be spiritually alive and on fire by the Holy Spirit.

- *The congregation consists of believers who, by using the means of grace (the Word of God and the Sacraments) and the gifts of the Spirit (charismata) as directed by the Word of God, seek salvation and eternal blessedness for themselves and for their fellow men.*

Members of the congregation need to be true believers—that is, persons with personal living faith in Christ who are concerned for the salvation of others. The means of grace—that is, the Word of God and the sacraments—along with the gifts of the Spirit, have been given for our own salvation and as means for sharing salvation with others. The charismatic grace gifts of the Spirit are vital for the life of the church. We at North Heights are committed to using the means of grace (the Word and Sacraments) and the gifts of the Spirit (charismata) to lead the lost to salvation in Christ and to build up believers in their faith.

- *Members of the organized congregation are not, in every instance, believers, and such hypocrites often derive false hope from their external connection with the congregation. It is therefore the sacred obligation of the congregation to purify itself by the quickening preaching of the Word of God, by earnest admonition and exhortation, and by expelling the openly sinful and perverse.*

We seek to make it clear that church membership in itself does not make one a true believer. The message of sin and grace is necessary to lead to repentance and faith.

- *The congregation governs its own affairs, subject to the authority of the Word of God and of the Spirit, and recognizes no other ecclesiastical authority or government over itself.*

This principle expresses North Heights' relationship with denominational affiliation. Our church does not go along with the drift in church and society. I have expressed my convictions with each of the presiding bishops of the ELCA and with our own local bishops, with whom I have had an open door and a respectful relationship. Often I felt like a voice crying in the wilderness. Yet our congregation had complete freedom with no interference by church officials, even when we gave little or no financial support to our denomination. My desire was to speak the truth in love. Without compromising our convictions, I believe it is possible to disagree without being disagreeable.

- *A free and independent congregation esteems and cherishes all the gifts of the Spirit which the Lord gives it for its own edification and seeks to stimulate and to encourage their use.*

"Free and independent congregation" certainly describes North Heights. Some in our denomination consider us "maverick," and so we are. You could say that we are "non-conformists," and so be it. We do not follow the leader or vote with the majority very often. The description from our founding fathers aptly described us.

The use of the gifts of the Spirit are to be esteemed and cherished by the congregation and are to be encouraged for edification and ministry, our founding fundamental principles state. We have sought to do just that at North Heights, and the employment of the spiritual charismatic gifts has truly enriched the personal lives of many of our members and of our corporate life.

It amazes me that more than a century ago, prior to the Pentecostal outpouring in 1900, our denominational leaders endorsed, and even encouraged, the use of all the gifts of the Spirit for the upbuilding of the congregation and its members. However, they later rejected the Pentecostal movement for its high emotionalism and excesses.

"Every free congregation, as well as every individual believer, is constrained by the Spirit of God and by the privileges of Christian love to do good and to work for the salvation of souls and the quickening of spiritual life, as far as its abilities and power permit. Such free spiritual activity is limited neither by parish nor by synodical bounds."

The major task of the congregation is to work for salvation of souls and for stirring of spiritual life. The Holy Spirit is absolutely necessary for fulfilling this commission. There is no limit to the power of the Holy Spirit and to what He desires to do through us. There should be no limit then to what we do as we follow the leading of the Spirit. To these principles we subscribe wholeheartedly.

A Fellowship of Believers Empowered by the Holy Spirit

In his account of the Lutheran Free Church, Clarence Carlsen enumerated several of the foundational concerns: "personal Christianity, spiritual awakening, witnessing by the laity, evangelism, a democratic ministry, and a church life which follows as closely as possible the pattern set forth in the New Testament."

Stress was laid on personal assurance of salvation through faith in Jesus Christ, on purity of life and conduct, on witness and missions, and on freedom and independence of congregations. All these emphases helped shape my understanding of the gospel and of church life, and they have been essential in our congregation.

Georg Sverdrup, president of Augsburg College and Seminary, was the moving force in the founding years of the Lutheran Free Church. He stated that the congregation is essential to Christianity, and no other external organization is to be above or in addition to the congregation. Next to a concern for personal salvation, nothing is more important than the need for restoration or recovery of apostolic congregations. Originating with Pentecost, the congregation is a body and fellowship of believers empowered and guided by the Holy Spirit for the purpose of seeking and obtaining eternal salvation for themselves and others. To accomplish this objective, God has given His Word and sacraments together with spiritual gifts, which are crucial for the spiritual development of living congregations.

Sverdrup's convictions about active faith, spiritual gifts, and living congregations describe clearly the heart of North Heights and the directions all of its pastors were seeking during their pastorates. These ideals and truths shaped North Heights' DNA from the beginning, and they have described the spiritual development of its members.

In 1961 the life histories of North Heights and Morris Vaagenes merged. The blending of the two journeys of faith shaped the lives of both for the next four decades. What had been my experiences in the walk of faith? What was the life message and ministry the Lord was writing on my heart? How would these impact my ministry at North Heights?

Before You Were Born I
Consecrated You

Chapter 3

Now the word of the Lord came to me saying,
"Before I formed you in the womb I knew you,
and before you were born I consecrated you;
I appointed you a prophet to the nations."
(Jeremiah 1:4-5)

I was eleven years old when I was asked for the first time what I wanted to be when I grew up. My answer was matter-of-fact and without hesitation, "A missionary!"

Of course, I was going to be a missionary. I had not given thought to a life vocation before, but it was there in an unconscious state. The Lord had already written it on my heart. At that moment, it found expression for the first time. From that day on, there was never a doubt. No other vocation ever entered my mind. The location of my missionary service was never a question, either. Of course, it was to be Madagascar.

A Family Affair

Why a missionary? Why Madagascar? The answer was obvious. My parents were missionaries to Madagascar, and it was there that I spent eight years of my childhood as a missionary kid (MK).

The call to missionary service seemed to be in my family bloodline. My father was born in 1888 on the island of Radøy just north of Bergen, Norway. He was christened Mons Gjerten Karlson. His parents were participants in the spiritual awakening movement which stretched across Norway. It had its roots in the evangelistic fervor of Hans Nilsen Hauge in the early 1800s and the revival that sprang up as a result of his ministry. While my grandparents remained members of the Lutheran State Church of Norway and participated actively in their parish church, much of their spiritual nurture was received at the weekly meetings held in the local Prayer House (*Bedehus*) and in their home devotionals. Prayer houses, which were lay led, dotted Norway's countryside and served as local spiritual awakening centers.

From an early age my father sensed that God was calling him to be a missionary, and at the age of twenty he applied to the Norwegian Mission Society's Missionary Training School at Stavanger, Norway, to prepare for that call. He was one of forty-four candidates applying for sixteen openings, but sadly he was not among those accepted. He asked his pastor what he should do, since he felt he had received a clear call from God to be a missionary. "Go to America, to Augsburg Seminary in Minneapolis!" was his pastor's immediate reply.

At that moment, my father felt an outpouring of the Holy Spirit flowing through his whole being, and he sensed that this was the Holy Spirit confirming the call to be a missionary and directing him regarding training. I would add that I believe it was the Spirit anointing my father with power to fulfill the call on his life.

But he needed a further witness. He must have his widowed mother's affirmation as well, since he felt a responsibility for her and his younger sisters. He was ten when his father had died, and at the time of his missionary call, he was the oldest child at home. How would his mother feel?

My father went home and told her what had transpired, his rejection by the Missionary Training School, and their pastor's recommendation to go to America for his education. He asked for her counsel and blessing. She said, "God has called you and you must go to America!" It was a deeply moving moment for mother and son.

A Time of Consecration

My father went out to their farm field which overlooked a fjord and in the distance the Atlantic Ocean. He gazed as far as his eyes could see and tried to imagine his destination across the vast expanse of the ocean far from home. He thanked God for the call to missionary service and for the double confirmation to go to America for his training. He consecrated himself wholly to the service of the Lord, and he released his mother and his sisters, whom he would leave behind, to the care of the Lord. Once again, as he was in prayer out on his farm field, he felt the waves of the Holy Spirit flowing through him as before.

The very next day he said his farewells to his mother, sisters, and other relatives, and then departed for England and the United States. It was with tears and torn hearts that they parted. The next and only time he would see his mother again was twenty years later on his way from Madagascar to America on his first furlough. The year of his departure from his childhood home to go to his new home country was 1909.

Nearly 100 years later, in July of 2006, I visited the farm where he grew up, as I had done on several previous occasions. This time I walked out and stood on the highest spot of the field where my father had prayed that day so long ago. It was a moving moment for me as I sought to recapture what was going through his mind and heart almost a century earlier. As I stood there I thanked God for the way He led my father and mother, and for their obedience to the heavenly call. I expressed gratitude for their faithful service in the Lord's vineyard. It was a time of personal consecration to God's continuing call in my life.

After working in building construction in Racine, Wisconsin, where his brother Cornelius lived, my father moved to Minneapolis to study at Augsburg College, graduating in 1916, and at Augsburg Seminary, graduating and receiving his ordination in 1919. By this time, he had become a naturalized citizen of the United States and had Americanized his name to Morris George Carlson Vaagenes, taking the farmstead name as his family name.

In 1920 he left for language study in France. Madagascar was a French colony and French was the official language. He studied at Grenoble University in the city of Grenoble in the French Alps. In 1921 he sailed for Madagascar.

God Prepares My Mother

My mother, Hanna Bøvre, was born on April 8, 1893, in Biri, Norway, not far from Lillehammer where the 1992 Winter Olympics were held. Her parents were pious Christians and were active in the local Prayer House (*Bedehus*). Her father was a farmer, saddle maker, musician, and lay preacher. As was the case with my father, my mother was ten when her father died. Two years later, her mother left for America with the two younger children to seek work to support her family since opportunities in Norway were very limited. Her best chance at finding work in America would be as a housekeeper on a farm, and that would be easier with two children rather than three. Therefore, my mother was left in Norway and lived with her grandparents. In 1907 at the age of fourteen, she left Norway and joined her family in Wisconsin. Shortly after her arrival, she began working as a housekeeper to support herself.

At the age of seventeen while working for relatives in North Dakota, she was awakened to faith in Jesus Christ as her Lord and Savior. At the same time, she sensed the call to be a missionary. After attending Minnesota College in Minneapolis, she entered deaconess and nurses training at the Lutheran Deaconess Home and Hospital in Minneapolis. While a nurse at the hospital, she first met my father, who was preparing to be a missionary to Madagascar. They shared their common calling to be missionaries. She expected to serve in China. Little did they realize the plans the Lord had for them for their future, to serve together as a missionary couple in Madagascar.

The Lutheran Deaconess Home and Hospital and Augsburg College and Seminary were institutions of the Lutheran Free Church (LFC). Consequently both of my parents became members of that denomination. The LFC's foreign mission agency was called the Lutheran Board of Missions (LBM), and its two mission fields were Madagascar and China.

China was closed to missionaries at the time my mother applied to serve as a foreign missionary. As a result, she was called to Madagascar to serve as a nurse for Dr. John Dyrnes in Manasoa. Dr. Dyrnes, a medical doctor and ordained pastor, began his missionary service in 1900. By the time my mother arrived to serve as his nurse in 1923, he had already become a legend because of his extensive medical, educational, agricultural, and evangelistic activities.

Malaria was a major health issue both for natives and missionaries. Almost from the commencement of the LBM mission work in southwest Madagascar, a number of new missionaries fell ill with malaria in its most acute form, Black Water Fever, and died in their first years in Madagascar. My parents were not spared from this dreaded disease in their early years on the mission field. While still single missionaries, each of them were stricken with Black Water Fever, but by God's grace they were saved from death.

A Family in God's Service

It was at a missionary conference that my parents began a relationship that led to marriage in 1926. Four children were born into their family. Carl was born in Madagascar in 1927, and I was born in America in 1929 while they were on furlough. My two sisters were born when we returned as a family to Madagascar, Adelaide in 1933 and Lois in 1935.

The year before Lois' birth, Carl left for Fort Dauphin, 250 miles from our home in Betroka, to attend the American Lutheran Missionary Children's Home and School. He joined three-dozen other missionary kids who were all in the same boat, far from home and separated from their families.

Carl was six years old, and I was four, when he left home for the first time. The "good-byes" were always hard. It was especially difficult for Carl because for the first time in his life he was separated from his family. Besides, he knew none of the other children before arriving at the boarding school. To add to his struggles was a language factor. At home our parents made us speak English at mealtime, but Carl and I talked Malagasy when we played together, and we used Norwegian when we prayed.

Before going to school, we were more fluent in the Malagasy language than in English. As a result, Carl had greater struggles in English than did the other children.

As for me, I lost my best friend and playmate, my brother. Carl came home twice a year for vacations. Otherwise, we did not see him for close to five months at a time. As Adelaide grew older, she became my dear friend and playmate.

Two months prior to my departure for school at the age of six, Carl, Adelaide, and I came down with measles. For Adelaide, the illness progressed into pneumonia. Penicillin had not yet been discovered, so there was no effective cure for pneumonia at that time. As Adelaide was lying on her deathbed, she sang and hummed hymn after hymn, some fifty different ones, my parents recounted. She was only two-and-a-half years old. It was like an angel singing. She had learned the hymns by attending ladies aid meetings with my mother. My mother would teach the women hymns by rote, since few could read. Adelaide learned the songs before most of the women, and the songs she sang in her last hours on earth were all in the Malagasy language.

It was late afternoon on January 6, 1936. As death drew near, my father told Carl and me to go to our room and pray for Adelaide. After we had been praying for some time, he came into our room to tell us that Jesus had taken our little sister home to sing in His heavenly children's choir. How sad we were! A hole was left in my heart, an emptiness that still exists today. How I miss Adelaide! I can't speak or write about her without being overwhelmed with sadness.

Word of her death spread quickly in our town. Church members and government officials came to our house to express their grief.

Adelaide's body was placed in our living room. Mourners paused there to grieve her passing. Many Christians remained in our house and on the verandah surrounding our missionary residence. They sang one hymn after another, verse after verse, all from memory. Some stayed all night, intermittently singing and sleeping. How comforting it was for me, a young six-year-old boy, to fall asleep to the beautiful sound of Malagasy hymns sung in four-part harmony!

Early the next morning we viewed Adelaide's body for the last time. The picture of her beauty is still indelibly inscribed in my mind.

The whole church gathered at our house for the procession to the church. Carl and I, still quarantined with measles, were not able to attend our sister's funeral service. We watched out the window as her body was carried away in a little wooden casket that our carpenter had made after her death. My parents walked behind the bier, followed by French government and business officials, and by Abela, the pastor of our Betroka Church, and by church members and townspeople. They sang hymns as they proceeded to the church. All Carl and I could do was watch and mourn. Tears streamed down my face as I could only look on from a distance.

Our mother read stories of heaven with us from the book of Revelation and from the Visions of Heaven by Sadhu Sundar Singh, a well-known Christian leader in India. In our imagination we could picture our dear sister in heaven with Jesus and with the angels. What a comfort that was for us!

School and Another Tragic Loss

Seven weeks after Adelaide's death, I went with Carl to Fort Dauphin to start first grade at the MC Home and School. I was six years old. That was my first time apart from my parents. I always kept my emotions hidden, so it was only natural that I held my feelings of loneliness in check. Nevertheless, I did feel homesick at times. One Sunday afternoon I was lying sick in bed with malaria. I could hear another missionary kid (MK) playing "Home Sweet Home" on the piano in the room below mine. This was the favorite song of the children because it expressed the loneliness each one felt. As I listened to the song, I was homesick for my parents who were 250 miles away. I missed my mother's loving touch during that time of illness. Living away from home could at times be very painful, but all of us in the MC Home and School were in the same boat. This led to a deep bonding with the other children. The missionary kids became like brothers and sisters, and the missionaries were considered as uncles and aunts. The American Lutheran missionary community became a big family, and I was part of it.

After my first five months at the MC Home and School, Carl and I went home for a short vacation. While we were there our one-year-old sister, Lois, contracted diphtheria. My parents took her to the local hospital, where the French doctor gave her an immunization shot for diphtheria. This was a tragic medical error. When Carl and I awakened the next morning, we were told the sad news that Lois had died during the night. She was the baby of the family, and the youngest is always special to parents and older siblings. Another sorrowful vigil, funeral and burial! This was August 13, 1936.

I am sure that the experience of the loss of my two sisters and the separation from my parents at such an early age has impacted my life and ministry significantly. I have deep empathy for those who lose a loved one, especially a young child, and I feel the pain of those who are lonely due to separation from loved ones or who are without family. I have compassion for those hurting emotionally and physically.

My Early Spiritual Influence

My first three years of schooling in Madagascar were formative in shaping my worldview and the direction for my life. There was no separation of secular and sacred. It was all one, and God was at the center. I loved the school. I loved the other MKs. I loved Madagascar! I loved the people! I loved the Malagasy Church! I loved being a missionary kid! I loved the Lord!

Devotions were an integral part of our dinner meal. My father's prayers covered the globe, and included our relatives in Norway and the U.S., the Malagasy church, the mission work and missionaries, the mission board, Augsburg College and Seminary, the LFC leaders, pastors and churches, and much more. To a young boy my father's prayers seemed awfully long, although I never complained. They broadened my vision of God's activities and of the world.

One daily prayer request I will never forget was his plea for revival—in our Betroka district, in our mission field, in the church in Madagascar—and in each of us as well. There has been a long history of revivals in Madagascar, all indigenous dating from 1896. The effects of earlier revivals continued on for generations. The seeds of revival were sown into my heart at an early age and have remained there ever since. The longing in my heart has always been for revival, beginning in me and extending to whatever churches I was serving.

My father was involved in casting out demons, and evil spirits are certainly prevalent in that land of animism, the worship of spirits. Exorcism has been an important ministry in all revival movements, along with healing, prophecy, and miracles. My parents believed in healing and miracles, and I grew up hearing stories of the supernatural. As a result I have had no problem believing that God still works wonders today.

A Move to the States

In 1939, our family left Madagascar for what we thought would be a one-year furlough. We spent the summer in Europe, mostly in Norway visiting relatives. We arrived in New York City two days before World War II began. We were staying in the Bronx when on September 1, I was awakened to the shout of a newsboy crying, "EXTRA, EXTRA! READ ALL ABOUT IT! HITLER INVADES POLAND!" The world would never be the same again. Demonic forces would wreak global havoc and devastation. Tens of millions would lose their lives because of the war. Cities and nations would experience massive destruction. Six million Jews would be annihilated in gas chambers. Communism would rise out of the ash heap of the war and seek world domination. Two billion people would be imprisoned by its hammer and sickle.

The island of Madagascar, situated off the southeast coast of Africa in the Indian Ocean, was isolated from outside forces. Life was primitive and simple. As a child, I knew next to nothing of life and events on the world scene. Suddenly, at the age of nine I was thrust into a world that seemed to be going crazy.

The contrast for me was dramatic. In Europe and the United States I was thrust into marvels I never imagined existed. For instance, my eyes must have been huge in amazement as I walked along the exquisite wide tree-lined *Avenue des Champs-Élysées* in Paris, and as I stood under the Eiffel Tower, and walked through the grand Arc de Triumph where many famous conquering generals and their armies marched.

Then later, after crossing the Atlantic Ocean, I joined hundreds of other passengers who lined the deck rail of the Norwegian ocean liner *Stavangerfjord* as we entered the New York City Harbor. I was struck by the sight of the Statue of Liberty, the great symbol of the United States of America, a symbol of freedom for millions of immigrants coming to a new land of opportunity. How amazed I was as I craned my neck in Manhattan, overwhelmed by the large number of mighty skyscrapers. As we drove past the Empire State Building, I looked up in utter astonishment at the height of that landmark.

At the 1939 New York World's Fair, I stood awe-struck as I was introduced not only to the modern world of that day, but was also shown the "World of Tomorrow." In my childhood in Madagascar, I had never experienced electricity or other aspects of modern life, which were taken for granted in America. What a leap of time and cultures I was experiencing!

Due to World War II we were unable to return to Madagascar. We lived in our church's missionary residence in south Minneapolis for the next four-and-a-half years. The cultural and moral environment in America into which I was thrust, quite innocent in comparison with today's standards, differed significantly from the untainted setting I knew in Madagascar.

Preparations for My Life's Calling

The next fifteen years, from age nine to twenty-four, were marked as a time in which the Lord was preparing me for my calling to be a missionary. During that time I completed my elementary and secondary schooling, as well as my college and seminary education—all in Minnesota.

Many persons and events impacted my development during this time of training. My parents, more than anyone else, were the most influential. My father was my role model for life and ministry. My mother nourished much of my personal development. Both of them were dedicated, warm-hearted, pietistic believers who brought us up to place our full trust in the Lord and to live our lives in keeping with the Word of God. They lived what they taught.

Our home church, St. Luke's Lutheran Church, was five blocks from our house in Minneapolis and provided a good setting for my spiritual nurture. Besides participating in worship services, Sunday school, vacation Bible school, confirmation and Boy Scouts, our family also attended the weekly Wednesday evening prayer meetings and late Sunday afternoon fireside services. Carl and I were the only children at the latter two events. Yet, we never protested going to these adult events.

I held the pastor of St. Luke's, Dr. Claus Morgan, in the highest regard. He served as a role model in my pastoral ministry. He was entrepreneurial. He birthed many different ministries and was especially supportive of foreign missions. He grew the church from a small congregation to one of the largest in our denomination. He gave leadership to several local, national, and global organizations. He had longevity, serving as pastor of the congregation over a span of forty-eight years.

Dr. Morgan was my confirmation teacher. He met with each of the twenty-eight members of my class on a personal basis to inquire about the individual's relationship with the Lord. In my conference with him, he asked some general questions about my faith and life. He must have assumed that everything was right between me and the Lord, but I knew differently.

During the confirmation service, one issue kept going through my mind. Following the service, we were to go to the church basement where people would come and greet us. I was afraid that someone would ask me what my confirmation meant to me. I didn't know what to answer. I had memorized much of the catechism and knew the Bible stories, but as to my personal faith in Christ I did not have an answer yet. Throughout the service I was trying to figure out what to say if this question would be posed. I couldn't come up with an answer. Fortunately, no one asked me. My dilemma led me in my pastoral ministry to make sure that with every confirmation class I taught, all the children would know the meaning of their confirmation, and especially what Jesus meant to them.

A strong work ethic and entrepreneurial spirit developed in me early in life. At eleven, one year earlier than the requirements, I had my first paper route. Within a short time, I took over the adjacent route in addition to my own, thus doubling my customers. Delivering eighty-five papers every afternoon and on Sunday mornings at 4:00 a.m. was not easy. In addition, collecting money from some on my route was like pulling teeth. I learned commitment and endurance at an early age.

My father traveled across the Upper Midwest and Pacific Northwest speaking in churches about mission work in Madagascar. After two years of deputation work, he served as pastor of five rural churches near Thief River Falls, Minnesota. Since there was no parsonage for the pastor and his family, my father stayed at members' homes while we continued to live in the missionary furlough home in Minneapolis. Due to the need for nurses during the war years, my mother worked at the Lutheran Deaconess Hospital in Minneapolis. Carl and I knew how to fend for ourselves, even as we had learned from an early age at the MC Home in Madagascar.

In late fall of 1943, my father was approached about serving as pastor of three churches in the Madelia area, ninety miles southeast of Minneapolis. The pastor wanted to serve as military chaplain at a Lutheran Service Center, and thus needed someone to take his parish for the duration of the war. This worked out perfectly for our family.

We spent the next two and a half years in this town of 1,500. This was the first extended family time that we had known since I was six years old, when Carl and I left for boarding school in Madagascar. I had a more settled feeling inside me, and I'm sure that it was because of the close relationship with our parents.

My Need for a Savior

My spiritual quest found fulfillment at Bible camps and Luther League conventions. It was at Camp Koronis Bible Camp that I came to see my need for a Savior. It was on a Tuesday evening in response to Dr. Merton Strommen's message that I asked Jesus to come into my heart and be my Lord and Savior. I gave my first testimony to faith in Christ at the campfire service that night, quoting 2 Timothy 1:12: "But I am not ashamed, for I know whom I have believed, and I am sure that he is able to guard until that Day what has been entrusted to me." Then I said that I had given my life to Christ that night at the chapel service, and I had a new peace in my heart. Dr. Strommen, who led the campfire singing and sharing gave me a supportive smile. I was glad that I had taken that step of faith and had borne witness to Christ.

Later that night, I asked my roommate if he wanted to commit his life to Christ. He said that he was not ready to do so. Fifteen years later, I read in the newspaper of his tragic death. He was working on the demolition of a building in downtown Minneapolis when a big safe that was being lifted from an upper floor broke the chains holding it plunging through several floors and crushing him. I trust that he did come to personal faith in Christ at some time in the intervening years. This incident impressed on me the tremendous importance of responding in faith to the Holy Spirit's invitation to yield one's life to Christ.

In retrospect, I recognized that Jesus had been my Savior from the time of my baptism in childhood. I came to see that as my spiritual life was being nurtured by my parents and at the MC Home and in church, my faith was developing from an unconscious state into greater consciousness. My experience at Bible camp was not a conversion, but an awakening to Jesus as my personal Savior and Lord, and my response of surrender.

Bible camps and national youth conventions, led by our denomination's youth director, Dr. Merton Strommen, were like heaven on earth for me. Those times were my spiritual highs, when my faith was most fervent. My attitude and behavior were vastly different following these holy seasons. I joined the Pocket Testament Movement in which I committed to read the Bible daily and carry a portion of Scripture with me wherever I went. I memorized a new Bible verse every day. But I found my fervor and faith waning between these high points, partly because of a lack of fellowship with other Christian young people.

My spiritual experiences and faith understanding during my teenage years have shaped my ministry to children and youth. I see the great significance of bringing up children to know Jesus personally at the various levels of their development. Parents are the prime nurturers for their children. In the early teen years, and partly as a result of reaching puberty in which the sexual drive emerges and new temptations arise, young people become conscious of their sins in a way they did not realize before. They are most open to receiving forgiveness for their sins through Jesus' substitutionary death on the cross. They are self-conscious and seek their identity through peer acceptance. What they need is a peer group that is committed to Christ and God's Word, and a church youth ministry that provides spiritual guidance and support. Above all, they need to find their identity and acceptance through God's love for them as seen in Christ and given them by the Holy Spirit.

In 1946 at the conclusion of World War II, our family left Madelia and went in three different directions. My parents returned to Madagascar where they were badly needed, , while Carl enrolled at Augsburg College as a freshman. I had two years left of high school, but I decided to skip my junior year and move into the senior class. I did not want to be separated from Carl for two years. My parents arranged for me to stay with a farm family in southwestern Minnesota, Otto and Sageng Tostengaard and their pre-school children, Luther and Ruth. Their farm was near Dovray in the Westbrook school district. The Tostengaards were wonderful people and treated me most graciously. I found good

Christian fellowship with the youth in their church and at the high school.

Period of Great Growth

Following my graduation from high school, I enrolled at Augsburg College. The atmosphere seemed to me like an extended Bible camp or Luther League convention. The prevailing spirit among the students was one of warm evangelical spirituality.

There were certain times where I felt my greatest loneliness. For instance, my parents were not able to be present at my graduations from high school, college, or seminary, nor were they at my ordination into ministry. There were no graduation parties or celebrations. Christmas Eve was possibly the most difficult time. This is the most family-oriented day and celebration of the year. But Carl and I had no family or home of our own where we could go. Our dormitory room was our only home. There were those who invited us to be with them, and we enjoyed being with them.

On one Christmas Eve after work at my part-time job at Swedish Hospital, I was invited to Carl's mother-in-law for dinner and gift opening. After the joyous celebration I returned to my dorm room. The large men's dormitory was empty. There were no lights on in any room. No one else was in the building that night. I felt lonely, and I missed my parents. But it was comforting for me as I thought about the first Christmas Eve, that there was no room in the inn for Jesus. He knew what it was like to have no place to lay His head (Matthew 8:20).

In 1948 Carl and I, along with two dozen students from Augsburg, attended the first Urbana Student Mission Convention held at the

University of Illinois-Urbana campus. The Spirit moved powerfully on us and the 1,294 delegates present. On our return to Augsburg we decided to meet each Sunday morning before church to intercede for mission work, and especially for revival in Madagascar.

A powerful spiritual awakening had begun in 1946 at Farihimena through Daniel Rakotozandry, a pastor in the Norwegian Lutheran mission field. He had spiritual discernment and authority rarely seen anywhere, some missionaries reported. The presence of the Holy Spirit was manifest so powerfully that those entering the village came under conviction of sin and were led to repentance. Healings, casting out of demons, and even raising from the dead were taking place. He battled serious health problems and died in 1947, but the revival impacted the whole country. Even after his death large numbers made pilgrimages to Farihimena and experienced transformation. We who gathered every Sunday morning at Augsburg praying for revival became part of what was transpiring on the other side of the globe.

The highlight of my collegiate experience came during my senior year when I was on the Religious Council and president of the Mission Society, the oldest, largest, and most active organization on campus. The first Lutheran missionaries of Norwegian descent to go out from America were sent out by the Augsburg Mission Society. The first missionary, John Hogstad, departed in 1887 and the second, Eric Tou, in 1889. Both went to Madagascar and became founders of the American Lutheran missions in the southernmost part of the island.

During my years at Augsburg, 15 percent of the students joined the Mission Society. The members were divided into teams, and these teams put on services twice monthly in gospel missions, churches, and nursing homes. Each group was comprised of a variety of musicians, speakers, and leaders. This practical experience provided excellent training for ministry. There were monthly meetings for the whole group with special speakers. We raised money from the students for support of mission projects.

One meeting stands out in particular. Our large group meeting for January 1951 was to take place on the first Friday night following the return of students from Christmas vacation. It was a short week of classes. Consequently, there would be little opportunity to publicize the meeting. The speaker was Mrs. Kim from South Korea, who had a very moving story. I was concerned for a good turnout so that many students would be able to hear her inspirational message and be impacted by it.

I decided to spend all night in prayer to plead for a good turn-out and a moving response. I was specific in my request. I asked for attendance and offering double that of the largest at any previous meeting. At five a.m. I felt peace that my prayer had been answered, so I slept for a few hours.

I went to the meeting hall early that evening. Students came in droves and packed out the Science Auditorium. The attendance was twice what I had requested, or four times more than our largest attendance at any previous meeting.

Mrs. Kim shared her story. Korea had been under Japanese occupation during World War II. She told of going to the Japanese parliament, called the Diet, and spoke to the members from the balcony, which was permitted. She gave a strong witness to Jesus Christ as Lord and Savior. She was arrested and put in prison. She was filled to overflowing with the Spirit and with overwhelming love, and the Spirit and love of God permeated the entire prison.

She shared her faith boldly to the prisoners and guards. As a result of her life and witness, hundreds gave their lives to Christ. Revival broke out in the prison, and the whole place was dynamically transformed.

It was a truly inspiring testimony. The spirit in which she shared her story was a manifestation of the presence of the Holy Spirit. The Spirit of the Lord was powerful and evident to all in the meeting. The offering was taken following her message, and it totaled twice what I had sought in prayer. I witnessed answers to my prayer far beyond my request and expectation. I experienced in a most dramatic way the power of prevailing prayer and the outpouring of the Holy Spirit in answer to intense intercession.

A Challenge to Be Filled With the Holy Spirit

Another experience during my student years stands out as an important part of my spiritual journey. A few of us went to the Minneapolis Auditorium on Saturday evenings for Youth for Christ rallies. Thousands of youth attended these gatherings. The speakers always concluded with an altar call for salvation. Often the speaker would continue pleading for the unsaved to come forward, but with only meager response.

One Saturday night Dr. J. Edwin Orr spoke. He was professor in the Fuller Seminary School of Missions and a leading authority and author on revivals. I sensed something quite different about him as he presented his message about the Holy Spirit and how one could be filled with His presence and power. When he extended the invitation, he did not plead and beg as so many did. But the Holy Spirit moved the hearts of young people to respond, and many more than normal came forward in response to the Spirit's inner call.

At the rally an announcement was made that Dr. Orr would be speaking Sunday morning at Bethlehem Baptist Church in downtown Minneapolis. I felt an inner compulsion to go and hear him. As he spoke that morning he explained that the Holy Spirit is a person, the third person of the Godhead, with all the attributes of personhood such as mind, will, and emotions, and that we can have intimate fellowship with Him. Furthermore, the Spirit earnestly desires to live His life in and through us, since our bodies are His holy temple. He expressed that it is God's will that we be filled with the Holy Spirit and for Him to do wonders through us. He encouraged all to surrender their lives to Him and to receive the outpouring of the Spirit.

I felt a strong tug within to respond that morning and to receive the filling with the Spirit in my life. But I hesitated and did not go forward. To do so might be costly as far as my calling. I asked myself, "What would this do to my career as a Lutheran pastor and missionary? Besides, this is a Baptist church. If I sought the filling with the Spirit here, how would that go over in my denominational setting?"

I was deeply moved, and had a strong inner longing to be filled with the Spirit. But I turned down the opportunity. The day would come, however, when this experience would become reality in my life, but not for another ten years.

The Two Shall Become One

Chapter 4

Then the Lord God said,
"It is not good that the man should be alone;
I will make him a helper fit for him."
(Genesis 2:18)

From childhood I had always been fascinated by spiritual realities. I believed in miracles, healings, casting out of demons, the spirit realm of existence, heaven, and angels. Reading about revivals had always stirred my heart with the longing for this in my own life. I believed in divine guidance, that the Lord reveals His will to those open to His still small voice.

In that regard, I had the conviction that the Lord would guide me to the one He had chosen for me to be my wife. I did some dating in college and seminary, but I waited for inner guidance as to the one the Lord had chosen for me. The college and seminary were on the same campus, which made it nice for single seminarians to look over the field. I did my looking, and there were many fine Christian young women, but the Spirit had not given the inner sense of a particular one for me.

Then in my second year in seminary a freshman girl in the college caught my attention. I pointed her out to Ted Berkland, my roommate, and said to him, "I'm going to go out with that gal." He asked, "What's her name?" I said, "I don't know." But I was determined to find out. Part of the homecoming celebration was an open house in all the dorms. This was my opportunity to find out her name. I knew which dorm she lived in, so I went through the rooms until I found her picture and saw her name.

That's all I needed. The next time I met her on the sidewalk at school, I said, "Hi, Bonnie!" Her roommate asked, "Who is that?" She answered, "Some creep who thinks he knows me." Little did she realize that she would marry that "creep" some day.

I found out other information about her later. She was a farm girl from near a little town west of Minot, North Dakota named Blaisdell. Her parents, Fred and Agnes Bieri, were farmers who raised grain, Black Angus cattle, sheep, and horses on a large ranch. She had two older brothers, Alan and Marlyn (Bud) and one younger sister, Sandra.

I paid my own way through college and seminary without outside aid. I worked hard and long hours during the school year and in the summers. The year I met Bonnie I was working at United Parcel Services (UPS) in Minneapolis. I handled all the funds collected by the drivers and accounted for its accuracy. My working hours were anywhere from four in the afternoon to midnight, and between Thanksgiving and Christmas from seven in the evening to seven in the morning, then with classes from eight in the morning until noon.

One Thursday evening in early November, shortly after discovering Bonnie's name, my work load turned out to be light, so I was through early. I called Ted Berkland and asked him if he would go with me to the Lutheran Bible Institute (LBI) for their spiritual emphasis week service that night. He agreed, and we went. I had the inner sense, I believe from the Holy Spirit, that I would see Bonnie there. And sure enough, she and her girl friends were there. Later, I found out that was the only time she had been to LBI.

After the service I asked her if she wanted a ride to Augsburg. She replied, "Sure!" Then she invited her friends, and they all piled into my 1951 Chevrolet four-door sedan. When we came to the dorm, I asked Bonnie if she would go out for a ride. She agreed. Ted had his eye on one of the girls and asked her. So the four of us went out for a malt and to get acquainted. On returning to her dorm I asked her out for the next night, and she said yes.

When she returned to the dorm, she asked the girls who I was. She hadn't even known my name. Upper-class girls told her my name and that I was a "middler" in the seminary. This may have been a shock to her, for she was only seventeen, a freshman, and I was an old man in my second year in seminary. She may have been surprised that a seminarian took an interest in her.

Thus was the beginning of our relationship. The third date was to a church in St. Paul where I was to preach at the Sunday evening service. I spoke on missions, and I said that I was going to be a missionary to Madagascar. I wondered if that would blow her away, but apparently not, since she continued to go out with me. She did not reveal to me until after we were engaged that she also felt the call to be a missionary.

Marriage and the Beginning of Ministry

After six-and-a-half years in Madagascar, my parents were due for a furlough. They arrived in Minneapolis and met Bonnie, my future bride. We had planned to get married after I graduated from seminary, probably in June 1954, but my father prevailed on us to move the date up since they would have to return to the mission field in April of that year. So we set the date for December 27, 1953, at Bonnie's home church in Blaisdell, North Dakota. My father tied the knot and the local pastor presided. This was the best thing that has happened to me other than my relationship with the Lord.

I graduated from Augsburg Seminary in May 1954. On June 12 I was ordained at Zion Lutheran Church in Thief River Falls, Minnesota during the Annual Conference of the LFC, together with eight other classmates.

I served as interim pastor for two months in a parish of six congregations in the Thief River Falls area, churches my father had served a dozen years earlier.

Then, in mid-August Bonnie and I said our farewells to family and friends, took a train to New York City, and boarded the passenger ship the *Queen Mary* on our way to France to study language in preparation for our mission service in Madagascar.

We spent a year in Paris in language study as part of a large group of Lutheran missionaries from America who were going to Madagascar and Cameroon. We shared beautiful fellowship and were of one spirit. Bonnie and other missionary wives had a private tutor while I studied with some of the other men at the Sorbonne University.

During our time in Paris, Bonnie gave birth to our first child, Lois Margaret. We gave her the name of my younger deceased sister. She was the delight of our lives. She was baptized by Pastor René Blanc at the Lutheran church we attended in our suburb of Le Perreux.

Mission Service in Madagascar

In August 1955 we flew to Madagascar to undertake our calling as missionaries. We studied the Malagasy language for one year and then were placed at our mission station. We were assigned to a fishing village on the west coast of the island along the Mozambique Channel, a wide body of water separating Madagascar from Africa.

There had been no resident missionary at St. Augustine for a number of years. This gave us the opportunity to expand the outreach of the gospel into new territory. The first six months everything seemed to be advancing so beautifully. We were elated. Then suddenly reality hit. We discovered that many of those we trusted were not honest with us. As is their practice they told us what we wanted to hear. When we realized that we were being deceived, we became discouraged and depressed. Just at that time fellow missionaries Milo and Edie Gudim came to visit us. They were going through the same culture shock, and we were able to console each other and be more realistic after that.

In October 1956 our second child was born at the mission hospital at Manambaro. We named him Paul Luther. Within a few weeks after Paul's birth Bonnie noticed that there was something wrong. His head leaned to one side, and the condition kept getting worse. We consulted a French doctor in a larger city near St. Augustine. His initial thought was that his tendon on the one side needed stretching, but he referred us to the chief surgeon at the hospital. That doctor took an x-ray and discovered that Paul had a severe case of congenital scoliosis—curvature of the spine. He strongly recommended that we return to the United States as soon as possible. Then he asked where we were from in the states. We replied, Minnesota. He said that we could not have been from a better place, and he recommended the Mayo Clinic as the top medical center in the world.

The report that Paul had a serious case of scoliosis and that we needed to go to America for his treatment came as a terrible shock to us. We immediately called Caleb Quanbeck, the superintendent of our mission. He agreed that we needed to go back to America to get medical treatment for Paul. We consulted with our mission doctors as well, and they gave us the same counsel.

This was a major disappointment for us. Missionary service was our life calling. My whole family was in Madagascar at the same time. My brother Carl and his wife Ruth were also there as missionaries. But we knew that Paul's medical care must take first priority.

My parents were stationed at Betroka where I had lived as a child. They brought the prayer request for Paul to the revival people in their church, who after praying suggested that we take Paul to the capital, Tananarive, to the national revival leaders for prayer for his healing.

We decided against that for practical reasons and because of a certain skepticism regarding his getting healed. The French doctor had indicated that we needed to leave as soon as possible. The earliest flight we could get was in one month. To go to the capital for prayer would delay our departure by a week. To make reservations before going to the capital in case he was not healed would show lack of faith. So we did not go for prayer for healing. We can only guess at how our lives might have been altered had we gone for healing prayer and the Lord would have healed Paul.

Back to the Minnesota

We arrived back in Minneapolis on June 12, 1957, and both Bonnie and I had a strong sense of defeat. The missionary call in that era was a lifetime call, and here we were returning after only three years. It was a guilt we placed on ourselves. Our intention was to return to Madagascar, and so we left most of our belongings out there. As it turned out, Paul's medical care was long-term, so we were unable to return except for short-term mission trips.

We were able to get Paul into Gillette State Hospital for Crippled Children in St. Paul, a hospital founded in 1897 to care for children suffering from physical deformities and disabilities. Paul was eight months old when he entered Gillette, and was placed in the nursery until he was a year old. We were not allowed to see him other than through a window pane. Up to this time he had been with us constantly. Suddenly, he was taken from us and could have no contact with us for another four months. After that, for most of the next two years Paul was in a ward with many other children his age. Visiting hours were only on Saturdays and Sundays, and that for only a two-hour period. The staff was very strict in holding visitors to the allotted time.

Paul must have felt abandoned, but he never complained. He was the most patient of the children, and thus was well liked by the nurses. The person he most related with in the hospital was a black cleaning lady. They became the best of friends. For Paul this was natural, for in Madagascar the ones he had contact with were the native people of color.

When Paul was one year old, he was released to come home with us for two weeks. At first he was afraid of his mother. He resisted her attempts to hold him and cuddle with him. Then Bonnie realized the cause of his fears. He had been separated from us for four months without any contact. The persons who held him and cared for him were the nurses. So Bonnie put on a white dress and placed a handkerchief on her head to look like a nurse. Then he warmed up to her immediately.

In spite of the severe restrictions placed on parents regarding personal contact with their child, we were very grateful that Paul could have the top-notch care he received. The Twin Cities was the world's leading scoliosis center and Doctor J. H. Moe, his surgeon and physician, was considered one of the top three globally in this field.

Dr. Moe performed surgery on Paul, fusing nine vertebrae in his upper back. Paul was fourteen months old, the youngest in medical records at the time for having such a surgery. Normally this surgery is performed on children in their late teens when they have quit growing. Paul's case was such that Dr. Moe felt they could not wait. Other children with conditions similar to Paul's, but who did not receive surgery, all died years ago. Paul is still alive at the age of forty-nine. He has had further surgeries on the cervical vertebrae and is disabled, yet is living a productive life doing volunteer activity with Love Lines, a Christian telephone counseling ministry, and with the healing and freeing from addiction ministry of Vision of Glory Lutheran Church in Plymouth. Paul and his eleven year old daughter, Sarah, live with us, which we count as a rich blessing. We thank God for extending his life these many years.

A Call to Pastor

After returning from Madagascar I did deputation work, speaking on missions in churches across the upper Midwest. At the same time we were open to a call to serve as pastor in a church in the Minneapolis and St. Paul area so we could be close to Paul in Gillette Hospital. That call came from the rural Christiania and Trondhjem parish in the Farmington and Londsdale areas, thirty miles south of Twin Cities.

Norwegian immigrants settled in these areas in the late 1850s and 1860s. The churches had solid pietistic foundations and enjoyed glorious spiritual histories. In the 1880s Christiania was the second largest congregation in its denomination with over 800 members. In the 1890s both congregations experienced powerful revival. Lars Skrefsrud, a Norwegian missionary to the Santal field in India and a gifted speaker, preached several times in Christiania, sparking an awakening that lasted throughout that decade. The preaching and teaching ministries of Pastor Elias Aas contributed significantly to the awakenings. One result of the revival was that seventeen individuals from Christiania entered into pastoral ministry or went as missionaries to foreign mission fields in the following years.

But there was also strife among the churches in the rural Christiania community. At one time four Lutheran churches in the community were named Christiania. Around 1900 one of the four broke away from the congregation I was to serve half a century later, but it was short-lived. Two of the other churches comprised one parish or congregation with two sites. They both bore the name Christiania Lutheran Church, identified as the East Church and West Church, four miles distant from each other, and at that time members of the Evangelical Lutheran Church, a one-million member synod of Norwegian background.

The East Church was located one-tenth of a mile from our Christiania Lutheran Free Church. These two white frame churches with high steeples were located at a high point in the rolling hills of the area and could be seen for miles around. They were identified as the "Twin Churches." Shortly before our arrival in the community, the East/West congregation was preparing to celebrate its centennial. The night before the big celebration the church burned down. The Free Church congregation offered their building for the Centennial Service. Some Free Church members thought it ironic in that they contended that their congregation was the first and that the other congregation was jumping the gun.

We were told that some previous pastors of the two parishes were not on speaking terms with each other, yet they lived only half a mile apart on a rural county road. There had been major contention between the congregations at one point, and stubbornness prevailed at that time.

The Christiania and Trondhjem Lutheran Free congregations were at a low point when they extended a letter of call to me to serve as their pastor. They had been without a pastor for six months. Christiania was down to 200 members when we came, and Trondhjem, which at one time had hundreds of members, was at 60. The parsonage, located on a forty-acre farm a half mile behind the Christiania church, was in a run-down condition. The parishioners were discouraged. Our denominational leaders had been in no hurry to recommend a pastor to them. But since there was no other available position for me near the Twin Cities, they gave my name as a candidate.

The nearly four years we served this parish were a tremendous blessing for us. We were received warmly into so many hearts and homes, and we were accepted as part of their families. During our time of service in this parish each church grew 50 percent in membership. The giving multiplied many-fold, especially for missions. Two favorite topics that I enjoyed preaching were missions and stewardship.

One Sunday I mentioned in my sermon that there were two couples in our Lutheran Free Church who had applied to serve as foreign missionaries, but there was no money to send them. As I shook hands with the congregants at the close of the service, Earl Arneson, a businessman from South St. Paul with roots in the congregation, said to me, "How much will it cost to send out one of the missionary couples?" I calculated quickly in my mind and replied, "Four thousand dollars." He said, "Bill me for one."

Some days later when I went to his place of business, he gave me a check for one missionary. Then he said, "I want you to go to the stock yards to the pig area and look for Mr. Dokken, a broker. He will have a check for the other missionary." Earl Arneson had challenged his friend to match his contribution, which he did.

There was in effect no youth program in the two churches. Christiania had a number of young people, but Trondhjem had only two teenage girls when we arrived and they attended Northfield High School. Their closest friends belonged to Bethel Lutheran Church in Northfield, a small LFC church with very few youth. We started a Luther League incorporating the three churches. We called it "The Tri-League" and it became one of the more dynamic youth programs in our denomination.

Church On Fire

The neighboring pastor and his wife, Ray and Dorothy Haugland, became our dear friends. They chose us to be baptismal sponsors for one of their children. The good relationship we shared spilled over to our congregations. We worked closely with neighboring churches, all of which were Lutheran. We conducted joint evangelistic and youth meetings. Both churches provided players for a top-notch fast-pitch softball team. Ray Haugland was one of the best pitchers in the state. There was an atmosphere of peace, harmony, and unity among the churches and the respective members. Members in both parishes were pleased for their pastors' peaceful relationships and the churches' joint services and activities. "Blessed are the peacemakers, for they shall be called sons of God" (Matthew 5:9) was my motto.

The two churches in our parish undertook major repairs, remodeling and repainting the parsonage and church buildings. Each entered into expansion and building programs and fund-raising during the final portion of our ministry.

Bonnie was in her glory when she was gardening, as might be expected from a farmer's daughter. She had a large garden and did much canning and freezing of vegetables and fruit. Some farmers invited us to pick peas, beans, and corn before the harvesters from the canneries would come.

In 1959 Paul was discharged from Gillette Hospital after spending two of his first three years in in-patient care. He wore a full body Milwaukee Brace. He was not able to walk, so he scooted around on his back. Lois was down on the floor playing with him. On December 21, 1960, another member was added to our family. Timothy Jon was born at the Sandford Farmington Hospital. When he was a few months old, he almost died from pneumonia. How thankful we are to God for sparing his life and to Dr. Mueller who stayed at his bedside during the most severe crisis.

Also in 1960, my parents retired after forty years in missionary service. My father was seventy-three and my mother sixty-eight. They bought a home in Minneapolis, but soon went to Superior, Wisconsin, where my father served as interim pastor at St. Paul's Lutheran Church.

Just as North Heights had a spiritual history that helped form its personality prior to my pastorate, I too had life-shaping experiences that molded me for my future ministry in this dynamic congregation. In every marriage two people with diverse backgrounds bring their differences together to form a new union. Yet they remain two distinct persons, with each making a contribution to the other and to their corporate life. How would the union of North Heights with Morris and Bonnie Vaagenes transform both parties and shape the congregation? Read on for the unfolding of this drama.

But I want to make clear the remaining story is even more than about this union. It is His Story, for it is the account of the Lord building His Church. The amazing thing is that the Lord chooses those of no account as His instruments in constructing this body of believers. To Him belongs all praise and glory!

Church On Fire

"You shall be holy; for I the Lord your God am holy."
(Leviticus 19:2)

"God has made Christ to be our holiness."
(1 Corinthians 1:30, RSV, NIV)

From the time of my youth I was on a personal quest for a deeper spiritual life. During my ministry at Christiania and Trondhjem churches this search intensified. At the same time I sought further training for a future return to the mission field. In regard to the latter pursuit, I took several graduate courses at the University of Minnesota in the field of anthropology. I found them helpful in understanding other cultures, especially primitive ones like those among which we worked in Madagascar. Had I studied acculturation before going out as a missionary, I would have been more observant of the culture and would have made fewer mistakes.

By Works or by Grace?

More important to me than the study of acculturation was the desire to live a victorious Christian life. I had been striving to live an overcoming life on the basis of willpower, but with little fruit. This was the only way I knew—the way of more intense self-effort. My sermons emphasized what we must do: pray more, read the Bible more, give more, witness more, sin less, etc. But I could never do enough, and I could not overcome my sinful nature.

Some years earlier while in college and seminary, I had come to see how utterly rotten my sinful nature truly was. Then a few years later a pastor friend of mine, Morris Johnson, hit the nail on the head when he declared in a message, "You are your own greatest problem." I realized that my problem was not other people and not my circumstances. My problem was my sinful nature. I could not run away from my problems. Since I was the problem, wherever I went, my problem followed.

I found that no amount of surrender, dedication, or commitment could overcome my sinful nature. Yet I kept hearing and reading that I must do more, try harder, surrender more completely, believe more strongly, and that this was the way to a victorious Christian life. Unfortunately, in much of the Christian church, the "self-effort" message seems to be the predominant and prevailing approach to a godly life.

For years I had engaged in a losing battle against my sinful flesh and Satan. I often felt depressed because I could never be good enough. One day I felt led to read a book that the dean of Augsburg Seminary, Dr. John Stensvaag, said that every pastor should read on an annual basis. It was entitled *The Quest for Holiness* by Adolph Köberle, a German Lutheran theologian.

Köberle writes of the futility of all human attempts to attain communion with God through such means as:

- The sanctification of conduct by the strengthening of the will.
- The sanctification of the emotions by a strenuous training of the soul.
- The sanctification of thought by a deepening of the understanding.

- Moralism, mysticism, or speculation, which he explained are the three ladders on which men commonly seek to climb up to God.

Köberle goes on to explain that the only means of acceptance before God is by faith in Christ's atoning sacrifice. He states that many who base their salvation on faith in Christ and not on works they must do, nonetheless seek to live the Christian life by human effort—that is, by increased zeal and determination. He demonstrates from Scripture that sanctification, like justification, is based on God's grace as manifest in Christ and must be received by faith. And he shows how the Holy Spirit is vital for us to fully understand this truth and live a victorious Christian life.

He writes: "Since all the words of penitence and thanksgiving, of supplication and intercession remain nothing but an empty river bed as long as the Spirit of God does not flow through them with His power, *the chief object of prayer remains the petition for the gift of the Holy Ghost*" (italics added).

Köberle makes clear the need for obedience to God's commands: "That the belittling of the duty of obedience is no small matter but of terribly serious importance becomes evident through the fact that there is nothing in the world that so completely destroys man as disobedience towards God." He adds that obedience is possible only because of the atoning sacrifice and obedience of Christ and the presence of the Holy Spirit: "Without the reality of the presence of the Holy Ghost such commands would be utterly meaningless. But ... God has turned tasks into gifts in the Gospel."

Church On Fire

A Liberating Revelation

This was news to me, good news. For the first time I came to see that a holy life is not achieved by human effort, no matter how diligent one might be, but it is a gift of grace to be received and lived out by faith. As a staunch Lutheran, I had to be convinced by Scripture and the Lutheran confessions. I came to a theological understanding concerning the Christian life. But how is this to be lived out in one's life?

One morning while still struggling with my sinful condition I sensed the Lord telling me to read Romans 7. As I read the second half of the chapter, I was amazed at how on target it was! It expressed my struggle perfectly! Later I called the Romans 7 way of trying to live a Christian life, the *I DO* way, which leads to *I DO NOT*—in fact, *I CANNOT*. In this chapter *I*, *ME*, and *MY* appear 52 times:

> *We know that the law is spiritual; but I am carnal, sold under sin. I do not understand my own actions. For I do not do what I want, but I do the very thing I hate…. So then it is no longer I that do it, but sin which dwells within me. For I know that nothing good dwells within me, that is, in my flesh. I can will what is right, but I cannot do it. For I do not do the good I want, but the evil I do not want is what I do…. So I find it to be a law that when I want to do right, evil lies close at hand…. Wretched man that I am! Who will deliver me from this body of death? (Romans 7:14,15,17-19,21,24)*

This described perfectly the battle raging within me. I recognized that in spite of all the willpower I could muster, it was not enough to conquer sin. This reality left me miserable and depressed, disgusted with myself. I cried, "O wretched man that I am!" That was me—wretched! I asked the same question Paul asked: "Who will deliver me from this body of death?"

The next verse popped off the page and struck me like lightening: *"Thanks be to God through Jesus Christ our Lord"* (v.25). Who can set me free? God can, through Jesus Christ our Lord! More than that, God not only can deliver me, but He has done it through Jesus. This was life-giving revelation to my heart!

I looked in the margin of my Bible for cross references. The first one I looked up was 1 Corinthians 15:57: *"But thanks be to God, who gives us the victory through our Lord Jesus Christ."* I focused on each word and phrase:

- *"But!"* This key word was in contrast to the power of death spoken of in the previous verses. In answer to my problem of sin, defeat and my condition of death, I can respond, *"But!"*

- *"Thanks be to God!"* I saw that this was another way of saying, "Thank you, God!" The greatest prayer of faith is, "Thank you, God!" It is our response of receiving, believing, and declaring what God has given. As I meditated on this truth, I simply sighed, *"Thank you, God!"* I don't have to do anything to receive except to say, "Thank you, God!"

- *"Who gives!"* This indicated to me that victory is a gift of grace from God. We do not have to struggle or strive for it. He gives it as a free gift of grace. "Gives" is in the present tense, which in Greek is a continuous present, which means that *God is continually giving us victory.* Every time

I looked at that verse, I noticed that God was still giving. Praise the Lord!

- *"Us!"* This included me. "Thank you, God! You are giving *me* this victory!"

- *"The victory!"* This is not just any victory, but *the* victory, the *only* victory, *Christ's victory.* God does not give us, or me, defeat. He gives us victory—Christ's victory. Thus, *His* victory becomes *my* victory. I have no other victory but Christ's. I declared, "Jesus, you are my victory!"

- *"Through our Lord Jesus Christ!"* Our only victory is through Jesus' triumph over the devil, the world and our own flesh. Our victory in Christ is complete victory. Therefore, I proclaimed, "Lord God! I thank you that you have given me the victory of our Lord Jesus Christ."

I repeated this verse to myself over and over until it penetrated into my inmost being. Every time a thought of defeat or depression would hit me, I declared with firmness: *"But thanks be to God, who gives me the victory through our Lord Jesus Christ!"* Through continuous proclamation of this truth, negative thoughts would fade. In the following weeks, I repeated this verse numerous times daily. A pattern of victory was being established in my spirit, in my mind (both conscious and subconscious), in my will, and in my emotions.

I put to memory other passages that impacted me positively:

- "But thanks be to God, who in Christ always leads us in triumph, and through us spreads the fragrance of the knowledge of him everywhere" (2 Corinthians 2:14).

- "I can do all things in him who strengthens me" (Philippians 4:13).

- "Little children, you are of God, and have overcome them; for he who is in you is greater than he who is in the world" (1 John 4:4).

- "For whatever is born of God overcomes the world; and this is the victory that overcomes the world, our faith" (1 John 5:4).

Not Legalism, But Love

Out of the revelation of our victory through Christ's triumph, a life-message was being formed in me, that of the victorious Christian life. It is Christ's life exchanged for my life. It is not so much a "changed" life as an "exchanged" life. I cannot live the Christian life. The good news is that God exchanged my failed life with Jesus' fruitful life. The Christian life is not striving to live a better life. It is simply receiving Jesus' life to replace my life. This life is not something I do, but a work God has done in Christ, and now wants to do in me. Thus, the Christian life from beginning to end is a matter of grace and not law. It is freeing, not burdensome. It is neither legalism nor license, but love.

"Legalism" is trying to live the Christian life by rules or human effort, leading to frustration and failure. "License" is abandoning law and allowing the sinful human nature to express itself freely without restraints. "Love" is the fruit of the Spirit's control in one's life. The Holy Spirit reproduces Christ's life in those who yield to His guidance. The Christian life is gospel—it is good news. Unfortunately, this truth is one of the best kept secrets in the church!

I do not claim to be living a victorious life on a consistent basis. By no means! I fail too frequently. Thankfully, I have discovered that one's life message is forged out of areas of personal weakness and struggle into which God reveals His solution in Christ. Through the years, I have been tested again and again, and even in those areas where the Lord dealt with me earlier. His purpose is to lead me to a deeper and firmer foundation in that truth and to a greater reliance on Him.

My quest for holiness and the discovery I received has transformed my life and shaped my message significantly. I include it in some detail here and in a later chapter because this truth and subsequent revelations from the Bible became a major element in my ministry and in the shaping of the North Heights congregation.

Come Over To North Heights
Chapter 6

And a vision appeared to Paul in the night:
a man of Macedonia was standing beseeching him
and saying, "Come over to Macedonia and help us."
And when he had seen the vision,
immediately we sought to go on into Macedonia,
concluding that God had called us
to preach the gospel to them. (Acts 16:9-10)

In the spring of 1961, I received an invitation to speak at North Heights in that they were considering me as a candidate to succeed Pastor Cal Storley, who had been called to serve as Youth Director of the LFC. I accepted the invitation to preach a "trial sermon", as was common in that era. "Trial" it was both for the preacher and the congregation.

God's Glory and Grandeur

I spoke at a Wednesday evening Lenten service, and my text was Psalm 8, not a normal text for Lent. I was captivated by the grandeur and glory of God in the light of the vast universe:

> *O Lord, our Lord,*
> *how majestic is thy name in all the earth!*
> *When I look at thy heavens, the work of thy fingers,*
> *the moon and the stars which thou has established;*
> *what is man that thou are mindful of him,*
> *and the son of man that thou dost care for him?*

I spoke of the vastness of the universe, seemingly without end. Our earth is just one planet in our solar system, which in turn is just one of hundreds of million of stars in our galaxy the Milky Way. This is just one galaxy in the universe composed of hundreds of millions of galaxies each composed of hundreds of millions of stars. And to think that the nearest star outside of our solar system is 4.5 light years—or 25 trillion miles—away from us! Within 100 light years of earth there are only 25 stars. This is astounding. How utterly awesome is our God, the Creator of it all.

If we think this is mind-boggling, we see another world also outside of the visible realm—that is, the world inside of a particle. All matter consists of particles, which are comprised of atoms. An atom is not visible to the human eye except under an atomic microscope, yet within an atom there is tremendous power. (For example, when split, the energy within an atom of uranium 238 is so great that it could send the Empire State Building soaring into space!)

All of this was created by our Almighty God and it is beyond comprehension. When I look at the heavens and consider the utter vastness of it and the incomprehensible complexity of the created order, I see myself as but a little speck of dust in relation to all of this grander and glory. Yet God has a different perspective on me and every human being. The psalmist continues:

> Yet thou hast made him little less than God,
> and dost crown him with glory and honor.
> Thou hast given him dominion over the works of thy hands;
> thou hast put all things under his feet.

Even more awesome than the utter vastness and complexity of the universe that God has created is the truth that He made us a little less than Himself, and He crowns us with glory and honor. He has made us to be caretakers over His created order. What a high calling and responsibility He has given us!

Our starting point and pivotal position in life is God and His created order. But since we have sinned and fallen far short of God's glory, we desperately need a Savior to redeem us from our sinful condition and to restore us to God's original intent. The good news is that God sent His own Son into the world to save us. He became fully human and fulfilled the Father's intent of reclaiming for us our dominion over His creation. Jesus accomplished this by making atonement for our sins on the cross and by restoring us to the position God intended for us through His resurrection, ascension and glorification.

In response to God's design in creation and Christ's work of redemption, what can we say but, *"O Lord, our Lord, how majestic is thy name in all the earth! How awesome is our God!"*

A Clear Call

I must have passed the test, for the congregation sent me a letter of call to serve as its pastor. This created a major struggle for me. What about the visions we had for the Christiania-Trondhjem parish where we were serving? What about the call the Lord had placed in us to be missionaries? Complicating our decision was the uncertainty of the length of Paul's medical treatment and the possibility for our return to Madagascar.

My immediate reaction was to turn down the call, but something in my spirit did not allow me to do so. I struggled for some time with the call. I didn't want to leave our parish, yet I couldn't say no to North Heights. Finally, I recognized that I must let go of my reasoning and will, and I must surrender the matter to the Lord. Turning the decision over to the Lord gave me peace. A few days later in my devotional time I received a clear impression that this was the Lord's will for us. The call to North Heights was possibly the clearest act of guidance I have ever received, and I needed it, as future events would indicate.

After sensing the clear direction to accept the call from North Heights, suddenly fear came over me. "It will be very painful to leave the wonderful parishioners in the Christiania and Trondhjem parish," I thought. "Will they feel that we were using them simply as a stepping stone to a larger church? What will this do to the fund drive and building program at Christiania? And will they call someone who will continue with the direction and the active youth ministry we have developed?" These were questions that troubled me.

"If I am calling you to North Heights," the Lord spoke into my mind, "don't you think I can bring the right pastor to this parish? Furthermore, if the churches and building program are built around you, they are constructed on a wrong foundation." He then reminded me of the scripture, "For no other foundation can any one lay than that which is laid, which is Jesus Christ" (1 Corinthians 3:11).

All I could say was, "Lord, you are right. I accept your direction concerning North Heights, and I surrender the Christiania and Trondhjem churches and people to you." Peace again filled my heart.

I called the joint council of the two congregations to the parsonage and announced my resignation. One member responded, "What will it cost to keep you?" I said, "I cannot be bought for a price. I do not even know what the salary will be at North Heights, for that is not a consideration for me. The determining factor is God's will, and we feel in our hearts that this call is from the Lord."

Parting is never easy, particularly where there is a positive love relationship, which we felt was mutual. We released the dear people of that parish into the hands of the Lord.

Now, forty-six years later these two rural churches continue to flourish, each with its own pastor. Furthermore, each one has been served through the years by able, dedicated pastors. The members remain committed to the Lord and active in His service. Trondhjem Church has grown a great deal in membership, and as a result purchased property just outside of Lonsdale to allow for expansion. They have built a new facility and expanded to it. The old church building has gone through a major restoration project and is now on the National Registry of Historic Sites.

Christiania Church, now renamed Highview Christiania Lutheran Church, has increased in membership also and has had two building expansion programs in addition to building a new parsonage.

We Move to North Heights

In response to this clear inner guidance, I accepted the call to North Heights. Bonnie and I thus stepped out in faith, not knowing what lay in the future but with the full assurance of who was directing our steps. And so on August 1, 1961, Bonnie and I, together with our three children, Lois, Paul and Timothy, moved into the North Heights parsonage next to the church and began serving this flock of 525 members. Our youngest child, Mark, was born one year later.

What a switch for us! We moved from a beautiful, isolated, quiet rural setting to the bustle and noise associated with living next to a major thoroughfare. Rice Street was a main highway for semi-trailer trucks hauling livestock from the north to the world-famous South St. Paul Stockyards.

The first weeks after we moved into the parsonage, the temperature hovered in the upper 80s and 90s, with the humidity nearly as high. The evenings were sweltering hot. At our previous rural parsonage, a grove of large trees shaded the house from the sun's heat. There were no trees to provide shelter in our new home. Home air conditioning was rare in those days. Our only means for partial relief was to open the windows wide. We were accustomed to absolute quiet in our previous isolated setting. But now, located on a major highway, it sounded like our bedroom was in the middle of the busy thoroughfare. All night long trucks roared by our house bringing loads of livestock to be sold in the morning at the stockyards. During the first couple of weeks we were miserable as we were deprived of sleep. Was this to be a sign of the heat and disturbance we were to experience in the years to come?

For Better or Worse . . .

We enjoyed a short one-month honeymoon with our new church. Then came big challenges—or more accurately, one breaking and crucifixion after another. Little did we realize the joys and struggles that would lie before us! Our relation with North Heights would be truly like a marriage union. We were linked together "for better, for worse; for richer, for poorer; in sickness and in health, until death do us part." We were wedded for the long haul. As with marriage, the real person emerges after the wedding ceremony and after the honeymoon is over. I'm sure the congregation was asking, "Who is this new pastor we just called?" Did we make the right decision? And we were wondering what we had gotten into.

On my first Sunday, some junior high boys decided to put me to the test. One of them had a buzzer in his hand. As he shook hands with me, the buzzer gave me a surprising shock. I laughed, and they laughed too. Thereby I was initiated into their group, and in their eyes I was all right. I passed the test. I accepted them, and they accepted me. Some of the boys' fathers, knowing what their sons had planned, were watching to see how I would react. I received their approval also.

The next test was far more challenging. It was in finances. Shortly after our arrival, the congregation voted to increase its indebtedness from $88,000 to $220,000 so as to construct a much-needed Parish Education unit. This debt figure was three times the criteria that lending institutions had established for churches. That did not stop the North Heights members. The service of Church Bonds, Inc. was engaged to assist in selling bonds to our members and to the general public.

This large debt load placed an extremely heavy financial burden on the congregation for the next dozen years. But at the same time it demonstrated the dynamic spirit of the people who dared to take such a giant leap of faith. However, when income did not meet the greatly increased expenses, I took personal responsibility for the shortfall. I felt the financial burden rested with me, and that I was not measuring up to the church's expectations of me.

Another major issue confronted the congregation three months after our arrival. This related to denominational merger. In the late 1950s, the LFC participated in merger negotiations with three other church bodies that led to the formation of The American Lutheran Church (TALC) in 1960. However, the LFC congregations in a 1958 church-wide referendum failed to approve the merger. The LFC Annual Conference authorized a second vote to be taken in all congregations during the fall of 1961. In this second referendum, North Heights voted 63 against and 62 in favor of the LFC merging with the ALC. Feelings in the congregation were strong on both sides of the issue, particularly by those opposed to merger.

In the 1961 referendum the required majority of LFC congregations approved merger. The union with the TALC was to take place February 1, 1963. What direction would North Heights take? It appeared that whichever direction the congregation would go, a significant number of members might leave.

What were the issues? There were two major concerns in the LFC and especially at North Heights. One was the prevailing or perceived spiritual emphasis or lack of it in the larger body with which we would merge. The other major concern was unbiblical direction and activities of the World Council of Churches (WCC).

There was a contingency in the newly formed denomination that shared views similar to the LFC on piety and spiritual life. Many North Heights members feared that the LFC's emphasis on personal faith and conservative theology would be overshadowed

by a liturgical, sacramental, liberal, and social gospel approach—
views which many in the TALC held.

The WCC leadership promoted liberal and liberation theology,
advocated peace and justice issues, and supported radical Marxist
revolutionaries. The TALC was a member church in the WCC. In
addition, many end times teachers held that the WCC would
become the end-time apostate church, which would enter into
alliance with the antichrist.

Some at North Heights feared that merger would mean moving in
the direction of liberalism and apostasy. Thus, they felt strongly
that they could not under any circumstance be part of this harlot
church. To be a member of a denomination which belonged to the
WCC was tantamount to being in the antichrist's apostate church.

Other North Heights members did not see it that way. They felt
that greater opportunity for witness would open for us by joining
the 2.3-million member national church body. The LFC churches
were mostly in the Upper Midwest and the Pacific Northwest. Our
influence would be far greater in the larger body than in our small
group, many held. Besides, other pastors and members in the
TALC shared our convictions. We could have fellowship with a
larger number of like-minded churches.

Early Building Projects

Even before the resolution of the merger issue, by an 85 to 15
vote the congregation decided to move ahead with its building
program. A beautiful parish education building was constructed in
1962. It included a narthex, offices, fellowship hall, fireside room,
nursery, and kitchen. It was a major step of faith, but it provided
much needed space for the growing congregation. This certainly

was another big challenge and a major step of faith for North Heights in the light of a possible split.

I was in favor of building, but at the same time I knew this would place even greater pressure on me. "How will we be able to meet these large financial obligations?" I wondered. "Even if the congregation would stay intact and not divide over the merger issue, our faith and finances would be stretched beyond the limits of human possibility. And if a split over the merger issue were to take place, we would be in a very precarious, even disastrous, position." I felt that we were in a humanly impossible situation. But that's good, for every miracle is birthed out of a desperate problem.

Many were involved in major roles in this project. Three principle persons were Walt Raleigh as building committee chairman, Art Suneson as construction supervisor, and Frank Berends as bond program director. Numerous others made major contributions.

In 1965 a garage and breezeway were added to the parsonage, thanks to the work of Art Suneson, Jim Schwartz, and others who assisted them. In 1967 the sanctuary was enlarged and a Moller pipe organ installed.

Unity of the Spirit

To those who had tasted the new life of the Spirit (more on that in the next chapter), the issue of merger with the TALC became a secondary issue. The new walk with the Spirit took precedent. Their joyous attitude spilled over to some others who were deeply concerned about merger and opposed to it. I kept quiet about the issue. I had my convictions, but I surrendered the matter to the Lord. I did not instruct Him how the vote should go. Instead, I left the matter with Him. While I was personally in favor of the merger, I struggled with what I should do if the congregation voted against affiliating with the merged denomination. Finally, I told the Lord I would go whichever way the congregation voted.

Many were apprehensive about the outcome of the vote, but a small group of us prayed at the altar for a spirit of love to prevail at the meeting where the issue was to be decided.

Then came the decisive moment! At the annual congregational meeting the third Tuesday in January 1963, a council member made a motion for our denominational affiliation in our constitution to be changed from Lutheran Free Church to The American Lutheran Church. The motion was seconded. The floor was open for discussion, but there was only prolonged silence. No one spoke. Vince Follmer, congregational president, gave ample time for anyone to speak. With no one asking to speak, he called for ballots to be passed out for the vote. The vote was counted, and the results were announced. The vote was 71 in favor and 13 opposed to joining the TALC.

The issue was settled. The decision was made in peace and love, two marks of the Holy Spirit. There was no dissention after the meeting. No small pockets of like-minded people gathered to talk about the vote.

Now the question some pondered silently was whether there would be a major exodus. As a matter of conscience, four families felt they could not be part of a denomination that belonged to the World Council of Churches, and so they left with sadness, but with good relationships maintained. With the merger question resolved, peace settled over the church.

Dependence on the Lord

The finances were tight throughout the decade of the '60s, due largely to the heavy debt load. A policy had been decided in the '50s that "the congregation will not engage in any activity for the sole purpose of fund raising." This was adopted so that responsibility for the support would depend on the members, not outsiders, and this through tithes and offerings.

We lacked sufficient resources for additional needed staff, so we were dependent on volunteers to give leadership and carry out the programs. That is not in itself bad, for it gives to members a greater sense of ownership. The volunteers did a terrific job. They are the heartbeat of the church. But when our membership doubled, it became more difficult for volunteers to devote the time required for greatly expanded programs.

At this time, charismatic renewal was becoming a sensitive issue in many churches. Some embraced it while others opposed it. Often a distinction and division arose between the "haves" and "have nots." In some places, pastors who introduced renewal into the congregation were forced to leave. In other instances, renewed members felt marginalized and even rejected, and eventually they left their church. Some congregations split over the issue. In our case, the Holy Spirit took a divided church and united it in love. This was unique and amazing. To God alone belongs the glory!

Every miracle comes out of a difficult situation in which human ingenuity is helpless. If it were humanly possible, it would not be a miracle. Every miracle is a release of divine supernatural power into a humanly impossible problem. When we come to the end of ourselves, the only place to turn is to God. I often felt inadequate and helpless. This was ordained by God so that I would not rely on my ability, but that I would see my total inability and place my trust in God. This is the story of my life. And this is the story of North Heights. Dependence on the Lord is a theme that runs through the account of my life and that of North Heights.

Church On Fire

My Soul Thirsts For Thee
Chapter 7

O God, thou art my God, I seek thee,
my soul thirsts for thee…. (Psalm 63:1)

On the last day of the feast, the great day,
Jesus stood up and proclaimed, "If any one thirst,
let him come to me and drink. He who believes in me,
as the scripture has said,
'Out of his heart shall flow rivers of living water.'"
Now this he said about the Spirit,
which those who believed in him were to receive;
for as yet the Spirit had not been given,
because Jesus was not yet glorified. (John 7:37-39)

I was into my first year as pastor of North Heights. Attendance was stagnant. Income was not sufficient to meet expenses. As a result, I declined a salary increase the congregation had voted me shortly after my arrival. I told the chairman of the board of trustees privately that I could not accept a pay increase in light of our deficit finances.

"Sacrifice by every member is called for to meet our financial obligations, and sacrifice must begin with me," I told him.

I took the lack of growth and financial shortfall as personal responsibility. Due to the heavy financial burdens of the congregation I did not receive a salary increase for some years.

Bonnie returned to Augsburg and got a degree in elementary education. She taught 6th grade for a dozen years at Brimhall School in the Roseville School District. In this way our financial needs were met, and Bonnie was able to express her love for children and for teaching. She made an outstanding impact on her students. At the same time she served on the church's Board of Parish Education, and she led and taught a Tuesday evening Bible study for women. Healing, growth, and maturity took place in many lives through her ministries.

A Place of Total Dependence Upon God

In various ways I felt I did not measure up to the members' expectations of me. Many longer-term members had come to personal faith and into membership through the ministries of my predecessors, particularly Pastors Kramer and Storley. This naturally resulted in deep gratitude and love for them. I had not been at North Heights long enough to gain their confidence and loyalty. It takes time to win people's trust.

In addition, I felt that I lacked the spirituality and personality of the two previous pastors. One old-time member, who later became one of my faithful supporters, said to me before my retirement from the church, "We didn't like you when you came." They missed their former pastors. Cal Storley told me later that when he came to North Heights he felt that he was not accepted during his first year. But he gained their trust and love, and was mourned when he left. Art Kramer had similar struggles.

I saw that I was unable in my own power to resolve these major challenges. I had not created the merger issue, nor could I resolve it. It was not my doing that led to an impending division over this issue. I came to see that the Lord was using these trying circumstances to strip me of confidence in my own ability to run the church or to solve problems. I realized that the Lord was bringing me to the point where I must depend solely on Him for all things and in all decisions. In Psalm 127:1, Solomon tells us, "Unless the Lord builds the house, those who build it labor in vain." Human wisdom and increased effort cannot avail. Jesus alone must be Lord of the church.

I recognized that the Lord was putting the squeeze on me. As a result, I surrendered myself, my ministry, my problems, and the church to the Lord in greater measure. I prayed, "Lord, you called me to North Heights. You knew the issues I would face. I didn't know them. Therefore this is your problem, not mine. This is your church, not mine."

How did the Lord deal with these tough situations? First, He dealt with me. I had to acknowledge that I—not others and not my circumstances—was my own greatest problem. When confronted with a difficulty, I learned the truth that the Lord was on my case. He was in the process of stripping me in some area of self-life so that He could replace it with His life. Invariably, my normal initial reaction was to blame adverse circumstance on others, not realizing that I was the problem that the Lord was dealing with.

I had recently come from a successful pastorate, and I took pride in what had been accomplished in my former parish. Now the Lord was teaching me that I was not capable of doing the work of ministry. He wanted me to acknowledge that I could not do it, and that I needed to get out of the way and let Him take over. The breaking process is always humbling and painful, but necessary.

Jesus said that "apart from me you can do nothing" (John 15:5). This is a difficult lesson to learn. Once I recognized this truth, then the Lord was ready to show me a second truth, probably equally hard to grasp, that "I can do all things in him who strengthens me" (Philippians 4:13).

An Increased Desire for God's Spirit

As I let go and allowed God to take over, I was introduced to the Holy Spirit in a new and more personal way. I knew Him theologically, that He is omnipotent, omniscient, and omnipresent. I believed in the Holy Spirit and saw evidence of His work in my life and in the church. Yet I knew there was more. I had prayed often to be filled with the Holy Spirit, but I felt it would be presumptuous to claim to be Spirit-filled. For years I had been seeking revival and manifestations of the Spirit's power as seen in the New Testament, but I saw little evidence of this. It seemed that revivals took place long ago or far from where I was.

As a teenager I had memorized Bible verses and whole chapters. One that impressed me strongly was Jesus' promise in John 14:12:

> *"Truly, truly, I say to you, he who believes in me will also do the works that I do; and greater works than these will he do, because I go to the Father."*

Added to this, He promised:

> *"I will do whatever you ask in my name, so that the Father may be glorified in the Son. If in my name you ask me for anything, I will do it." (John 14:13-14, NRSV).*

That promise must certainly include healings and miracles, I concluded. But why weren't they happening?

In 1959, prior to coming to North Heights, Bonnie and I sought earnestly for increased spiritual life and power in our lives and ministry. We prayed repeatedly for healing for our son Paul. In answer to our plea the Lord introduced us to the spiritual healing movement in the Episcopal Church. It was through conversation with Pastor Leland and Miriam Evenson at Lake Wapogasset Bible Camp that I came to hear about the healing and prayer ministry in what I viewed at that time as a very proper and stiff denomination. I knew Lee from the time of his youth as his family belonged to a church my dad served, and he had confirmed Lee. I knew Miriam from Augsburg College. He was pastor of a church in Lacrosse, Wisconsin, at that time, and later he had a long and highly successful ministry at Vision of Glory Lutheran Church in Plymouth, a western suburb of Minneapolis.

They recommended two books, *The Healing Light*, by Agnes Sanford, and *A Reporter Finds God through Spiritual Healing*, by Emily Gardiner Neal. The emphasis in these books and in the Episcopal spiritual healing movement was on the healing of the spirit and soul—that is, first a right relationship with God, then with oneself and others in which Christ is central. While physical healing is promised in Scripture, and is important, it takes second place to inner healing. Writes Mrs. Sanford in *The Healing Light*, "The essence of all healing is to become so immersed in the Being of God that one forgets oneself entirely." Emily Gardiner Neal reported with non-emotional precision about cases of miraculous physical healings by means of prayer, which were verified by medical reports from before and after the healings.

After careful examination, Bonnie and I concluded that these teachings and ministries were biblical, so we embraced the healing ministry and introduced it into our previous parish. We witnessed genuine miraculous healings through anointing with oil, the laying on of hands, and believing prayer. Of course, this does not diminish the role of medical science in the healing process.

For us, the spiritual healing ministry brought God's presence into our lives in a more conscious and manifest manner. We participated in a healing service in which a woman from a neighboring Lutheran church felt a burning sensation in the diseased area of her body when her pastor anointed her with oil and as we laid on hands and prayed. She was immediately healed from a physical condition which specialists at the University of Minnesota Hospital were unable to cure.

At that time, around 1960, most churches subscribed to the notion that the gifts of the Spirit had ended with the Apostolic Age. But upon closer examination, we saw no evidence in Scripture for the termination of spiritual gifts. Moreover, we were aware of extraordinary manifestations of spiritual gifts, particularly healings, exorcism, and prophecy in the awakening movements in the Lutheran Church of Madagascar. We wondered why churches in America and Europe virtually ignored the gifts, and why there was not an earnest seeking of the Spirit's life and power. There seemed to be a general neglect of the Holy Spirit in Western Christendom.

Through the healing movement in the Episcopal Church, we discovered not only the ministry of healing, but we learned that it was just one of many gifts the Holy Spirit offers. For the first time I met highly respectable people who spoke in tongues and affirmed this gift as a positive benefit in their Christian life. Prior to this time, every teaching and report I heard about speaking in tongues were negative.

Spiritual Gifts for Today's Church

One Saturday morning a few months after we had arrived at North Heights, the Rev. Oliver Carlson called me. He had heard that I was into healing and he wanted to find out more. Ollie was a longtime friend and associate. We both grew up in Madagascar and attended the American Lutheran Missionary Children's Home and School. Years later, Bonnie and I were together with Ollie and his wife Gene during language study in Paris, and then as missionaries in Madagascar.

That Saturday morning I shared my experiences with Ollie and told him about the spiritual healing movement in the Episcopal Church. I mentioned that I saw an announcement in the morning newspaper about a Spiritual Healing Mission that was to be conducted by Dr. William Standish Reed, chief surgeon at a general hospital in Michigan. This mission was to begin the next day at an Episcopal church in downtown St. Paul.

Dr. Reed spoke about the restoration of the healing ministry, and placed the healing gifts in context of the release of the Holy Spirit and of the charismatic gifts spoken of in 1 Corinthians 12 and 14. At the conclusion of his talks he invited people who were seeking healing to come forward for anointing with oil and the laying on of hands. He asked those who did not know Jesus as Savior and Lord to come and commit their lives to Him. And he extended an invitation for those seeking to be filled with the Holy Spirit and to receive the gifts of the Spirit to come to the altar for prayer. At a morning session someone asked him about speaking in tongues, and he spoke positively about it. This was the first time I heard someone with a position of authority and respect speak favorably about the gift of tongues. I took note.

I was already convinced that healing and other spiritual gifts were intended for the whole of church history and not simply for the apostolic age, as so many churches believed. For me the question was not so much the validity of the gifts of the Spirit in our time. My concern was in regard to the encounter or experience of being baptized with the Spirit. I could not accept this simply on the basis of Dr. Reed's word. I had to examine this issue on the basis of Scripture to see if it was biblical.

Do believers receive all the fullness of the Spirit in baptism? Or is this an additional experience we should seek? Is being filled with the Spirit part of spiritual growth and consecration? Is it a "second blessing" as some groups contend? What is the difference between baptism into Christ and baptism with the Holy Spirit—or are they the same? How about what the Pentecostals believe, that Christians need to be baptized with the Holy Spirit with the initial evidence of speaking in tongues?

My search of the Lutheran Confessions revealed a silence on the issue. To a Western Lutheran for whom systematic theology—or dogmatics—reigns as queen in theology, this was unsettling. I needed a clear, unequivocal, theological and biblical exposition which would make my theology indisputable. It seemed that if the scriptural account did not fit our well-ordered systematic theology, then we must adapt the biblical record to fit our theology, or else to disregard it as unclear.

On the other hand, having spent some years in Madagascar, I appreciated the Eastern worldview that sees existence from a holistic and more fluid perspective. I knew that in most cultures, from primitive to developed ones, "nonphysical realities have been seen as a more powerful influence on man's destiny than the physical world" (Morton Kelsey, *Encounter With God*,

Minneapolis: Bethany Fellowship, 1972, p. 42). This reality includes divine-human encounters, such as visions, revelations, miracles, and supernatural experiences. Since God chose to reveal and record Scripture through Hebrews who perceived reality through an Eastern worldview, I knew I needed to study and understand the Bible from that perspective.

In my study of the Bible I asked, "Is the outpouring of the Holy Spirit intended to be a biblical pattern for spiritual empowerment? Is such an experience central to the whole and heart of the Bible?"

What I discovered is that when God has a task to be accomplished, He chooses someone to do it, and He gives the power and wisdom to fulfill it. This power is the person of the Holy Spirit. Those whom God appoints, He anoints, and the anointing is with the Holy Spirit, thus enabling them to do spiritual work with the Spirit's gifts and in His supernatural power.

I noted that in the Old Testament and up to Pentecost, such outpourings were limited in time and scope to leaders such as Moses, the seventy-two elders, Joshua, the Judges, Saul and David, kings, prophets, and priests.

I found many prophecies indicating that in the latter days (i.e., the Messianic Age), the Spirit would be poured out on all, irrespective of age, gender, or social position. John the Baptist announced that Jesus would baptize with the Holy Spirit and fire. Jesus underscored the promise and instructed His disciples to wait in Jerusalem for its fulfillment. This empowerment took place on Pentecost Day, when they were all filled with the Holy Spirit and proclaimed Jesus' resurrection and Lordship with boldness. The outpouring of the Holy Spirit gave His disciples power and authority, which they lacked prior to this.

Furthermore, I noted in Acts that this Spirit-anointing experience was not limited to Pentecost, but was essential in the initiation of converts into the Christian faith. The steps of salvation included hearing the proclamation of the message of Jesus as the crucified and risen Savior and Lord. This brought conviction of sin and led to repentance and faith in Christ. The new converts were baptized in the Name of Jesus and through the laying on of hands received the gift of the Holy Spirit. In Acts the order varies, but this does not alter the importance of each act. Not all elements of Christian initiation are mentioned specifically in each instance of a conversion, but all are vital nevertheless.

I observed that when the apostles discovered one of the essential elements in Christian initiation had been omitted or was deficient, they quickly corrected the situation. This was true in Acts 8 in the case of the Samaritan converts, and in Acts 19 in the instance of the converts at Ephesus in which they had been baptized into John's baptism for repentance instead of into Jesus' baptism for regeneration. In both cases the apostles laid hands on individuals for the outpouring of the Holy Spirit.

I noted, too, that the initial outpouring on Pentecost Day (Acts 2) and on Cornelius and the Gentile converts (Acts 10) came by a sovereign act of God. But in the other instances, the impartation of the Holy Spirit was given through the laying on of hands. In the case of the Gentiles, Peter would never on his own initiative have laid hands on them or baptized them due to the strong convictions ingrained into him that the Hebrews were God's uniquely chosen people. They were to maintain a cultic separation from Gentiles, except for proselytes converted to the Jewish faith and law. It was only because of visions he received in which the message was communicated clearly—"What God has cleansed, you must not call common" (Acts 10:15)—and because of God's initiative in pouring out the Holy Spirit on the Gentiles, that Peter dared to baptize them.

I noticed further that several terms are used synonymously and interchangeably in Scripture for this enduement with the Holy Spirit's power. These include:

- *Clothed with power from on high.*

- *Baptized in or with the Holy Spirit.*

- *Filled with the Holy Spirit.*

- *Receive the gift of the Holy Spirit.*

- *Anointed/anointing with the Spirit.*

- *The Spirit falling on.*

- *The Spirit poured out.*

- *The Holy Spirit has come upon you.*

Each of these biblical term brings out a different aspect to the meaning of this overwhelming experience.

A Gift for All Believers

As a result of my examination of Scripture, I became convinced that it is God's will for every believer to be filled with the Holy

Spirit and to live in obedience to the Spirit's promptings. What God commands us to do, He provides the ability to accomplish through the Spirit's enabling.

The infilling with the Holy Spirit is a gift of grace. It is not earned, and it is not deserved, but it is a gift to be received by faith, as is emphasized three times in Galatians 3:

> Did you receive the Spirit by works of the law, or by hearing with faith? (v.3)

> Does he who supplies the Spirit to you and works miracles among you do so by works of the law, or by hearing with faith? (v.5)

> ... that we might receive the promise of the Spirit through faith. (v.14)

The reception of the Holy Spirit is not assumed in Acts, but is clearly to be appropriated by faith.

As I realized that the filling with the Holy Spirit is biblical, I began to earnestly seek the gift. Through prayer and the laying on of hands I received the Spirit's anointing. In retrospect I saw that I had received the indwelling Holy Spirit in my baptism, and recognized that the power of the Spirit had been poured out on me through the laying on of hands in my confirmation and ordination. But I did not understand on those occasions that the Spirit was given to dwell in me as companion and guide and to empower me for witness and ministry. I had prayed often to be filled with the Holy Spirit, but I did not know how to receive this gift by faith. I felt it would be audacious and arrogant for me to believe that I was Spirit-filled.

As I came to understand how to appropriate God's promises by faith, I asked for and accepted the Holy Spirit's filling and His gifts. Again in retrospect, I noted that many spiritual gifts had already been in operation in my life and ministry. I understood these gifts were to enable believers to perceive and minister in the spirit realm and with supernatural power. I came to see that the spiritual gifts, especially prophesy and the higher gifts, are to be earnestly desired (1 Corinthians 12:31; 14:1, 39).

Through my study of Scripture, I came to understand that the anointing with the Holy Spirit is essential for every believer for fruitful living and effective service in God's Kingdom. It must not be taken for granted. It is not optional. A way of stating the truth is this: the anointing with the Holy Spirit is the consecration, or ordination, of the priesthood of all believers for ministry. Ministry is to be accomplished in the power and wisdom of the Spirit. All believers are called to be ministers. The power needed to fulfill this calling is in the Spirit's anointing. The task of "ordained" ministers (pastors) is to equip "lay" (or consecrated) ministers to fulfill their ministry. The Holy Spirit's filling is both a crisis and a process—that is, an initial and a continuing filling.

Every believer is indwelt by the Holy Spirit, but not all are filled with the Spirit. The Holy Spirit is the Spirit of the Father and the Spirit of Jesus. He is also, in His own right, the Third Person of the Trinity. In receiving Jesus, a person receives the Father also, for Jesus and the Father are One. In receiving Jesus, a person also receives the Holy Spirit, for the Godhead is indivisible. Romans 8: 9-10 shows this truth:

> *But you are not in the flesh, you are in the Spirit, if in fact the Spirit of God dwells in you. Any one who does not have the Spirit of Christ does not belong to him. But if Christ is in*

you, although your bodies are dead because of sin, your spirits are alive because of righteousness.

We see here that having Christ in you is the same as having the Spirit of Christ and the Spirit of God dwelling in you. This indwelling of the Spirit, however, is different from the infilling with the Spirit. We observe this in Paul's letter to the Ephesian church. He addresses the readers as "saints" (1:1), in other words, as believers in Christ. Consequently, based on the above Romans passage, the recipients of this letter were *indwelt with Christ, the Spirit of Christ, the Spirit of God, the Spirit.*

Paul tells the believers in His epistle to the Ephesians that they "were sealed with the promised Holy Spirit" (1:13). To these believers who had already been sealed with the Holy Spirit, Paul wrote, "… be filled with the Spirit" (5:18). In the Greek text, this command is in the present tense, which is a continuous action. In other words, the command is to "be continually filled with the Spirit."

Scripture seems to make a distinction between having the Holy Spirit dwelling in you and the Spirit filling you. It's the difference between the Spirit residing in you and presiding over you, between the Spirit resident in you and president over you, or between the Spirit in you and on you and the Spirit inside you and beside you.

Jesus seems to make this distinction in John 14:16-17: "I will pray the Father, and he will give you another Counselor, to be with you for ever, even the Spirit of truth, whom the world cannot receive, because it neither sees him nor knows him; you know him, for *he dwells with you, and will be in you*" (italics added).

In the Greek text the name given the Holy Spirit here translated Counselor is *parakletos*, also translated "Advocate" in 1 John 2:1. It is a compound word: *para* meaning beside and *kaleo* meaning to call. As this word is used in relation to the Holy Spirit, we might say that He is the One called to be beside us. Scripture speaks of both Christ and the Holy Spirit interceding before the Father in our behalf (1 John 2:1; Romans 8:26). Advocate in French is *avocat*, from the Latin *advocatus*, meaning "lawyer" or "attorney." The term Counselor, or Comforter (KJV), pictures both Jesus and the Holy Spirit at our side to help, encourage, exhort, and comfort us.

Jesus said that He and the Spirit will continue to dwell or remain with you, and the Spirit will be in you. Formerly He had been with the disciples, but now, a reference to Pentecost when they would be filled with the Spirit, He would be in them. In the Old Testament the Spirit came on a select few to empower them for the work to which God had called them. But the Spirit entering into believers would take place in the age the Messiah would initiate, which began at Pentecost. The Lord prophesied through Ezekiel, "And I will put my spirit within you, and cause you to walk in my statutes and be careful to observe my ordinances." (36:27). In John 7:39 we read that "as yet the spirit had not been given, because Jesus was not yet glorified."

The inner presence of the Spirit indicates His inner sanctifying and guiding work in you and fellowship with you, while the outer outpouring speaks of the anointing upon you to empower you for service, witness, and ministry.

Having been convinced through Scripture that the filling with the Spirit is a genuine gift from God and is vital for spiritual ministry, and recognizing my deep personal need for the Spirit's power for my life and ministry, I sought this gift. During this time of searching and seeking, Ollie Carlson and I fasted and prayed together for the Spirit's outpouring in our lives.

"Thank you, Lord! I receive!"

The filling with the Spirit is a gift of grace, offered freely, apart from any work on our part. Yet to receive this gift costs everything we are and all we have. "There is plenty cost in Pentecost!" I said to myself. I knew I would be viewed as going off the deep end by friends and colleagues. This was considered very un-Lutheran. It might be viewed as Pentecostal, and at that time Lutherans looked on Pentecostals in a pejorative manner. Yet, my position and practice differed from that of Pentecostals. They held that speaking in tongues was the initial evidence of the baptism of the Spirit. I contended that the Bible does not support this view. In saying this I did not want to depreciate the value of and need for this gift. Every gift the Lord offers is good. At this point I had not received speaking in tongues. However, I knew I would be lumped with Pentecostals and thus considered leprous.

I had to lay aside all my inhibitions, as well as my ambitions for higher ecclesiastical offices and for other pastoral calls. I said facetiously that I was committing synodical suicide—that I would never get elected to any position in my denomination, nor would I be placed on the lowliest subcommittee of a subcommittee. But I was willing to pay the price. My prophecy has proven true with only one minor exception, but I have no regrets over what I gave up. What I received in return was much more fulfilling and rewarding. The Lord has blessed me far beyond anything I could ever have dreamed possible. Although at the time it seemed costly—to have my good reputation crucified and to become a leper—but I had no other option. So I gave it all up in order to gain this precious, priceless gift. Jim Eliot stated it well, "He is no fool who gives what he cannot keep to gain what he cannot lose."

One Monday morning in early spring of 1962, I went to pray in the majestic Cathedral of Saint Paul overlooking the city's downtown. I chose that place because I felt there would be too many distractions if I prayed in my own church. I spent several hours in the Cathedral, consecrating every area of my life to the Lord. With the Old Testament sacrifices in mind, I pictured myself at the altar of burnt offering, being crucified, and then laying every segment of my life on the altar to be consumed by fire. I needed to be emptied of self so as to be filled with the Spirit.

After laying my all on the altar of burnt offering, I went to the home of Evangelist and Mrs. Herbert Mjorud to seek prayer for the outpouring of the Holy Spirit. At that time, he was an evangelist in the Department of Evangelism for The American Lutheran Church.

Previously, I had misunderstood how to receive God's gifts and promises. Consequently, I had difficulty in accepting "the Spirit's enduement with power from on high". At various times I experienced definite manifestations of the Spirit's anointing, but I felt too unspiritual or unworthy to claim that I had the gift. I felt it would be presumptuous to say I am filled with the Holy Spirit.

Finally I came to the realization, based on Galatians 3:2,5, and 14, that the Spirit is received not by works of the law—that is, not by anything I do to earn this gift—but by hearing God's promises and accepting them with faith. It is by faith that we receive the promise of the Spirit. On the basis of God's word, I accepted by faith the Holy Spirit's filling in my life.

Church On Fire

An Awakening to the Spirit

Emotionally, I did not feel much different after I prayed, but I simply believed God's promise that the Holy Spirit was released in my life in a new way. I viewed it as my awakening to the Holy Spirit, just as at Bible camp at age 15, I was awakened to Jesus as my Savior and Lord. Jesus had been my Savior from my infancy when I was regenerated through baptism. But there at camp, through the unfolding of God's Word by Rev. Peder Strommen and his son, Dr. Merton Strommen, I understood, as I had not known previously, that my sins were paid for in full in Jesus' substitutionary atoning sacrifice. Thus, I accepted Him and His salvation as my own. In a similar manner, I knew that the Holy Spirit indwelt me from the time of my regeneration, but that day, I knew His Person and work in a way I had not previously known. I placed my dependence on Him and received His anointing power by faith.

What were the results of this awakening to the Holy Spirit? I had a much greater desire to read the Bible. It took on new freshness and meaning. The Holy Spirit spoke to me through Scripture in ways beyond my previous experience. Revelation of truths previously hidden from my understanding jumped off the Bible's pages and spoke to my heart.

Whenever I came across the Spirit's name in my Bible reading, I felt strangely warmed and my heart beat faster. I marked His name in purple for easy reference. I was falling in love with the Holy Spirit, even as I had fallen in love with Jesus at Bible camp.

In much the same way, my initiation into the healing ministry was a new awakening to the Father. I came to realize a further dimension of His love through His concern for my total wellbeing, including my physical health, and I came into a greater appreciation of His supernatural power through His healing miracles taking place now and not only in Bible times. I fell in love with Him in a fuller way. Thus, through these awakenings, the Father, Son, and Holy Spirit became closer and more intimate to me.

Furthermore, I realized I had approached the Christian life and service from a law or legalistic orientation, that is, that a holy life and fruitful service are dependent on my dedication, discipline, duty, and determination.

I came to the realization that Jesus has done everything necessary for me to overcome the devil, the world, and my own flesh. He accomplished this through His incarnation, crucifixion, resurrection, ascension, and glorification. The Holy Spirit revealed this truth to my heart. I trusted Him to work it out in my life as I believed His Word and obeyed His voice. I saw that this is available for all to receive.

It began to dawn on me that I was crucified with Christ on the cross two thousand years ago, and that I rose with Him and that now He lives His triumphant life in me as I walk in obedience to the leading of the Holy Spirit. I began to understand that a major battle is being waged inside me as a believer, a conflict between the Spirit and my sinful nature. To follow the Spirit's leading produces love, joy, and peace—the fruit of the Spirit.

The revelation of this truth lifted a heavy burden off of me, that of trying to live a victorious Christian life by my own efforts and zeal. Jesus carried the burden for me long ago. Now it is He who lives His life in me to the extent that I allow Him. My understanding of the Christian life shifted from "do" to "done"! It is not good deeds

I must do, but it is what Jesus has done through His atoning sacrifice and now desires to do in me through the working of the Holy Spirit in me.

Blessed With Every Spiritual Blessing
In The Heavenly Places
Chapter 8

Blessed be the God and Father of our Lord Jesus Christ,
who has blessed us in Christ with every spiritual blessing
in the heavenly places." (Ephesians 1:3)

On that spring day in 1962, after receiving the outpouring of the Holy Spirit, I left Herb and Gunhild Mjorud's home praising the Lord for this gift. I went home feeling jubilant. Actually, I went to my office at church. "That's one and the same place," Bonnie would say. I must admit that she was right.

As soon as I entered my study, I had a strong impression that I should read a certain book in my library. It was *Sit, Walk, Stand*, by Watchman Nee, an influential Chinese Christian leader who was imprisoned by the communist government for twenty years. I had purchased this short book a few months earlier on the recommendation of a pastor who said it was an excellent Bible study on Ephesians. I was always looking for good aids for adult Bible studies. So I bought it and put it on my bookshelf for future reference.

But now I had the distinct sense that the Holy Spirit was telling me to take it down and read it. Little did I realize that this little book was about to completely change my understanding of the Christian life and radically alter my approach to ministry.

The Essence of Christian Living

Ephesians expresses the essence of the Christian life in summary form, and *Sit, Walk, Stand* is the best study on the theme that I have encountered. Nee had the gift of stating truth in a clear, concise, understandable way, as you will observe in the following summary of his book.

Sit, the keyword in Ephesians 1-3, describes the starting point in Christian living and our relationship with God. Sitting is a position of rest. The Christian life begins with sitting, or rest. God has done all the work in Christ. When Jesus had finished the full scope of our redemption through His atoning work, God "made him *sit* at his right hand in the heavenly places, far above all rule and authority and power and dominion, and above every name that is named, not only in this age but also in that which is to come; and he has put all things under his feet and has made him the head over all things for the church, which is his body, the fullness of him who fills all in all" (Ephesians 1:20-23, emphasis added). Furthermore, God "raised us up with him, and made us *sit* with him in the heavenly places in Christ Jesus" (Ephesians 2:6, emphasis added).

The Christian's present spiritual position is one of sitting at God's right hand in the heavenly places in Christ Jesus. That was new to me. I had thought of it as future, that at the end of my life as a believer I would sit with God in heaven. But in this verse, *sit* is not in the future tense, but is a passive verb in the past tense, indicating an accomplished fact. God "made us sit." Right now, as a believer in Christ, I am seated in heaven in a place of victory "far above all rule and authority and power and dominion." The work of our redemption is completed.

Blessed With Every Spiritual Blessing
In The Heavenly Places

On the basis of Christ's finished work, God "made us to sit with him" in this place of victory. We are not even told to "sit," but to accept the fact that God has placed us in this position of rest in His heavenly presence. This is a present reality, not simply a future promise. The Christian life from beginning to end is Christ's work. And He has completed the work. We are simply to receive it, to abide in it, to sit down in Christ and enjoy it. This truth makes the Christian life gospel—or good news—and not law, or good deeds.

Walk is the key concept in Ephesians chapters 4:1 through 6:9. Our life in the heavenly places is to be walked out in our daily life on earth. This practical section expresses how we are to relate to the world:

> I...beg you to lead [**walk**] a life worthy of the calling to which you have been called.... (4:1)

> ... you must no longer live [**walk**] as the Gentiles do.... (4:17)

> And **walk** in love.... (5:2)

> Look carefully then how you **walk**.... (5:15).

Many Christians want to start the Christian life with walking, or doing, Nee explains. But in reality it begins with sitting, resting in what Christ has done. Only then can we learn to walk, for it is His life being walked—or lived out—through our lives. Nee states that every advance in our Christian walk begins with resting in Christ's completed work. The Christian walk is not one of striving, or struggling, but of resting in Christ, resting in who we are and what we have in Him. That was totally contrary to how I had been trying to live the Christian life.

Stand is the key word in our relation to the enemy (Ephesians 6:10-24). We stand on the ground of victory which Christ has won for us, Nee writes. If we forsake this position of victory and struggle for mastery over the devil, then we are already defeated. The apostle Paul tells us in Ephesians 6:

> Put on the whole armor of God, that you may be able to **stand** against the wiles of the devil... (v.11)

> Therefore take the whole armor of God, that you may be able to **withstand** in the evil day, and having done all, to **stand**. (v.13)

> **Stand** therefore.... (v.14)

Jesus defeated the devil through His crucifixion and resurrection. Jesus' victory is the believer's present possession, and not just a future hope. The believer needs to stand on this ground of victory and hold this position of triumph. That, too, was news to me— good news, God's gift, or gospel!

From Legalism to Grace

As I read *Sit, Walk, Stand*, I said to myself that this couldn't be true. It is over-simplification. "Nee is just picking out a few words and phrases and drawing false conclusions," I thought. To check him out, I read Ephesians, and then Nee, and then Ephesians, and Nee again, until the message started getting through to me.

I knew that we were justified before God by grace through faith, that Jesus purchased our salvation through His atoning work, and that we were to receive it by faith. But in regard to sanctification, or the Christian life, I understood that the believer's progress was based on one's dedication and discipline. What I heard and taught was this—that we must pray more, read the Bible more, overcome sin more, witness more, give more, go to church more, etc.

During my student years, I heard sermons by sincere evangelical and holiness preachers declaring that if you are not praying, you should pray at least five minutes a day. If you are praying five minutes, that's not enough; you should pray 15 minutes. If you are praying 15 minutes, that's not enough; you should pray half an hour. If you are praying half an hour, that's not enough; you should pray one hour. It all became a vicious legalistic cycle. I remember hearing on several occasions the example of Martin Luther who prayed two hours daily, and on days he was especially busy, he prayed three and four hours. Similar arguments were made for Bible reading, witnessing, giving and a whole host of other disciplines of the Christian life. In essence, these became legalistic rules for trying to live a victorious Christian life.

Somehow, according to this duty-based perception of the Christian life, a person can never do enough. Thus, according to this false teaching, our holiness is based on the measure of our diligence in fulfilling the Christian disciplines. That was what I had read in books on the Christian life and heard in many sermons. Thus, I was trying by sheer willpower to conquer sin and to overcome my sinful nature and the devil. But no matter how hard I tried, I could not win the victory.

In 1962, the lessons I was learning through Watchman Nee were building on those I had received earlier, that our victory is God's work from beginning to end. He has completed it in Christ and reveals it to us in Scripture by the Holy Spirit's inspiration. And now He wants to give it to us as a free gift of grace and to reproduce it in us. As we receive this gift by faith and obey the Holy Spirit's leading, He will manifest this life in us. Jesus is our victory and life. What a great mystery and wonder this is! This truth is discerned not by human reason but by divine revelation.

Dead to Sin and Alive to Christ

The next Watchman Nee book I devoured was *The Normal Christian Life*, based on Romans 1-8. Through this work, I came to the realization that each aspect of the Christian life is anchored in a specific act of Christ. For instance, forgiveness of sins is based on Jesus' blood.

Out of my subjective pietistic background, I had based forgiveness on my confession of sins, on the completeness of my confession, on my sorrow over sin, on my repentance, on my turning from sin, or on my restitution for sin.

But I found that the enemy of my soul would attack me with the accusation, "How can your quick prayer before bedtime, 'Forgive me all my sins,' bring forgiveness? Can a two-second prayer wipe out your sins of the day? That's ridiculous!"

So I would try to remember specific sins and name them. Again the enemy would come and accuse me: "Are you sure you named all your sins? How about this sin you missed and that one you didn't even know you did?"

And again he robbed me of forgiveness. And so I tried to feel sorry for what I had done. But my greatest sorrow was for those times when I got caught or someone else saw my sin. I couldn't work myself up into sufficient remorse for my sins in order to gain freedom from Satan's condemnation. Even restitution could not bring forgiveness and peace.

Yet these approaches were the ways I wrongly understood for receiving forgiveness. It is highly possible that this was not what preachers were teaching, but was due to my faulty perception.

To have a pastor pronounce absolution of my sins, i.e., to declare me forgiven, did not register with me. My misunderstanding of the Christian life was that I must do something to receive forgiveness and feel it subjectively. But like Martin Luther prior to his conversion, I could not arrive at the assurance of forgiveness on the basis of my action.

In *The Normal Christian Life*, Nee demonstrates that access to God and forgiveness of sins are based always and only on the blood of Jesus, using the apostle Paul's words in Romans:

> For there is no distinction; since all have sinned and fall short of the glory of God, they are justified by his grace as a gift, through the redemption which is in Christ Jesus, whom God put forward as an expiation [atoning sacrifice] **by his blood**, to be received by faith. (3:22-25, emphasis added)

*Since, therefore, **we are now justified by his blood**, much more shall we be saved by him from the wrath of God. (5:9, emphasis added)*

Old Testament blood sacrifices were types, pre-figures, and copies of the complete perfect sacrifice of Christ's blood:

*... he [Christ] entered once for all into the Holy Place, taking not the blood of goats and calves but **his own blood**, thus securing an eternal redemption. (Hebrews 9:12, emphasis added)*

*Therefore, brethren, since we have confidence to enter the sanctuary **by the blood of Jesus** ... let us draw near with a true heart in full assurance of faith, with our hearts sprinkled clean from an evil conscience and our bodies washed with pure water. (Hebrews 10:19-22, emphasis added)*

God forgives sins not by overlooking them, but by looking at the blood of Jesus. More than 200 times in both Old and New Testaments, blood is related to atonement for sins. The value of the blood is not based on our subjective feelings, but on accepting God's valuation of it.

Our confession of sins does not procure forgiveness. Rather, confession is an acknowledgment of our sins and the appropriation of forgiveness into our lives. The apostle John tells us: "If we say we have no sin, we deceive ourselves, and the truth is not in us. If we confess our sins, he is faithful and just, and will forgive our sins and cleanse us from all unrighteousness" (1 John 1:8-9).

When we confess our sins, two things take place. First, God forgives our sins, wiping our record in heaven clean. Second, He cleanses us from all unrighteousness, wiping our conscience clean. In both instances, the cleansing agent is the blood of Jesus, just as John reminds us that "the blood of Jesus [God's] Son cleanses us from all sin" (1 John 1:7).

The blood of Jesus has value not only with God and within us, but it has power against Satan. In Revelation 12:10-11, we are told that the devil accuses the believers day and night before God. We may add that he accuses us also in our own hearts continuously. How are believers to overcome him? John tells us that "they have conquered him by the blood of the Lamb and by the word of their testimony" (v.11).

We have a twofold victory over Satan's condemnations: the blood of the Lamb and the word of our testimony. We overcome Satan's accusations as we declare our faith in the power of Jesus' blood to forgive our sins and cleanse us within. Our trust is not in some subjective experience or feeling. It is exclusively through the blood of Jesus by which He has made full satisfaction for all our sins.

Prior to discovering this truth, my approach to forgiveness and to the Christian life focused predominantly on the subjective human response side of faith. Through Watchman Nee, I came to see the scriptural truth that faith must be anchored in Jesus Christ and His atoning work alone. Feelings fluctuate, but truth triumphs.

I saw further, as Nee points out, that I'm not a bad sinner because I commit many bad sins. I do many bad things because I am a bad sinner. It is my nature to sin. I was born a sinner. My sinful nature is due to heredity, and not behavior. I am a sinner because I am born of Adam. The only way I can be set free from my sinful nature and from the power of sin is through death.

God's solution to the problem of the sinful nature is to do away with the sinner. This He did in Christ's crucifixion. God put me, the sinner, in Jesus. When Jesus died, I died. I died to the power of sin. This is not something I have to do, but something that is already done. Paul wrote:

> *Law came in, to increase the trespass; but where sin increased, grace abounded all the more.... (Romans 5:20)*

> *What shall we say then? Are we to continue in sin that grace may abound? By no means! How can we who died to sin still live in it? Do you not know that all of us who have been baptized into Christ Jesus were baptized into his death? We were buried therefore with him by baptism into death, so that as Christ was raised from the dead by the glory of the Father, we too might walk in newness of life. For if we have been united with him in a death like his, we shall certainly be united with him in a resurrection like his. We know that our old self was crucified with him so that the sinful body might be destroyed, and we might no longer be enslaved to sin. For he who has died is freed from sin. But if we have died with Christ, we believe that we shall also live with him.... So you also must consider yourselves dead to sin and alive to God in Christ Jesus. (Romans 6:1-8, 11)*

In our death with Christ on the Cross, our sinful self was terminated. In Christ's resurrection, our new life commenced.

Jesus is our new life. To the measure we live in Christ and He in us, and to the measure we walk in obedience to the leading of the Holy Spirit, to that measure we are living in victory. To separate from Christ, or to see ourselves as separate from Him, leads to defeat. Victory comes as we see ourselves as one with Christ, as inseparable, in His death and in His resurrected life.

Not I, But Christ

As the truth of my oneness with Christ became more firmly established in me, my reading of Scripture was significantly altered. For years I had been misreading the passages dealing with what Christ had done for me, who I was in Him, and what I had in Him. I read them as what could be, if only I would measure up.

For example, Galatians 2:20 declares, "I have been crucified with Christ; it is no longer I who live, but Christ who lives in me; and the life I now live in the flesh I live by faith in the Son of God, who loved me and gave himself for me."

Here's how I understood Galatians 2:20: "I *ought to be* crucified with Christ; then it would no longer be I who live, but Christ who would live in me." Or I would read: "Get crucified with Christ, *dummy*, so that it will no longer be you who live, but Christ who will live in you."

Another rendition I had of this passage was this: "It is my goal to someday come to the point where I am crucified sufficiently that I can then say, 'I am to a large extent crucified with Christ; so basically it is no longer I who live, but Christ who usually lives in me.'"

One other way I understood it went like this: "Paul was so spiritual that he could say, 'I have been crucified with Christ; it is no longer I who live, but Christ who lives in me.' I hope and pray that I may be able to attain to that level of spiritually at some point in my life so I can say it also."

I mused, "Maybe when I am so old that the desires of my sinful body no longer function, then I might be able to say, with a shaky voice, 'I am almost crucified with Christ, and I am hardly living, but hopefully, Christ is living in me.'"

Honestly! These were my actual perceptions. My focus was on what I must do rather than on what God has done in Christ. I saw Galatians 2:20 as referring to my failure to live up to expectations, instead of my faith in God's Word. My attention was on me, not on Christ in me. It was on how I felt about my spiritual progress rather than on the fact of my spiritual position in Christ.

I had to come to the point where I declared as spiritual truth and as present reality, "I have been crucified with Christ; it is no longer I who live, but Christ who lives in me; and the life I now live in the flesh I live by faith in the Son of God, who loved me and gave himself for me."

This took place close to 2,000 years ago on the Cross. When Jesus died, I died with Him. So complete was my death that I was buried with Him. Since I died with Christ to sin's guilt and power, I need no longer live in bondage to sin. In my life in Christ, I am dead to sin. And since I rose with Christ to newness of life, I live, yet it is not really I who live, but Christ who lives in me. I live this new life by faith in God's Son who loved me so much that He gave His life in place of mine. Jesus is my new life.

To the extent that I let Him live His life in and through me, to that extent this truth is being manifest in me. When I choose to do my own thing, then it is my old "stinkin'" self living in me, and not Christ. As I recognize this return to my old self, I must again declare, "I have been crucified with Christ; and therefore, I put to death by the Holy Spirit's power this old self with its sinful desires, and I put on the Lord Jesus Christ as my life."

I must confess that too frequently I vacillate between the old life in the flesh and the new life in Christ. However, my failure does not negate the truth that I died with Christ to sin's control and rose with Him to His victorious life, and that I accept this biblical truth by faith and lay down all claims to my life so that His life may be lived out through me.

As I was learning these truths gained from scripture and Nee, and as I sought to apply them in my life by faith, I began teaching them in Bible studies and preaching them in my sermons. In essence, I was declaring the message to my own heart. However, I felt the teaching was going over the heads of the people, especially to the majority of attendees at the Sunday morning services. When I preached what I call this grace/faith message, I received little if any response after the service. I could understand why because it took me a long time to comprehend this message myself. In fact, for some years I would re-read Nee's books to be able to express the teaching clearly. There came a day when I did not need to go back to Nee, but now it became Me. If I reverted to a good old "law" sermon, I would get strong affirmation. It demonstrated to me that we prefer law to gospel. "Just tell us what to do!" seemed to be the human cry.

This Treasure in Earthen Vessels

I discovered another Watchman Nee book that had a profound impact on me. It was *What Shall This Man Do?* based on Paul's letters to the Corinthians. In these epistles we see Paul in his struggles and in his humanness. In chapter after chapter Paul defends himself against attacks by members of the Corinthian church. He opens his heart and life before them. He makes himself completely vulnerable. He boasts of his weaknesses. He explains that three times he prayed that God would remove a "thorn in his flesh," which was Satan's tool to harass him. Three times the answer came back, "No!" God said to him, "My grace is sufficient for you, for my power is made perfect in weakness" (2 Corinthians 12:9).

Paul responded, "I will all the more gladly boast of my weaknesses, that the power of Christ may rest upon me. For the sake of Christ, then, I am content with weaknesses, insults, hardships, persecutions, and calamities; for *when I am weak, then I am strong*" (vv. 9-10, emphasis added).

I was encouraged to see the struggles Paul endured and the difficulties he faced. He spoke openly and honestly about the practical aspects and struggles of his Christian life. Nee states that the Christian life can be pictured just as Paul states in 2 Corinthians 4:7: "But we have this treasure in earthen vessels, to show that the transcendent power belongs to God and not to us."

The Christian life is not simply the treasure, i.e., all the spiritual blessings in the heavenly places that are ours in Christ Jesus. Nor is it just the earthen vessel, i.e., the human dimension with its problems and weaknesses. The Christian life is the treasure in human vessels. This is the principle of incarnation (John 1:14),

Blessed With Every Spiritual Blessing
In The Heavenly Places

God coming in human form, and now Christ indwelling a clay pot—or as I like to say, a "crack pot." The mystery is that Jesus has chosen to live His life in common, ordinary, frail, weak earthen vessels. This is to demonstrate that God's amazing grace and all-surpassing power can overcome all obstacles.

"We are afflicted in every way, but not crushed; perplexed, but not driven to despair; persecuted, but not forsaken; struck down, but not destroyed; always carrying in the body the death of Jesus, so that the life of Jesus may also be manifested in our bodies. For while we live we are always being given up to death for Jesus' sake, so that the life of Jesus may be manifested in our mortal flesh" (vv.8-11).

The Christian life is not struggle-free. It is fraught with difficulties. This makes us dependent upon the Lord and not ourselves. Therefore while we rejoice in the hope of sharing in God's glory, "[m]ore than that, we rejoice in our sufferings, knowing that suffering produces endurance, and endurance produces character, and character produces hope, and hope does not disappoint us, because God's love has been poured into our hearts through the Holy Spirit which has been given to us" (Romans 5:3-5).

These were life-transforming truths that the Lord instilled into my heart in my early years in renewal. I spent most of my Mondays—my Sabbath rest—studying the Bible, absorbing Watchman Nee and reading other books which helped me in a paradigm shift from a largely introspective, critical, negative, law-oriented approach to a Christ-centered, forgiving, positive, loving, grace-filled mentality.

The Greatest Day of my Christian Life

I ran across a statement that expressed my discovery beautifully. It went like this:

> *The greatest day of my Christian life was the day I discovered I could not live it, and that God didn't intend me to. Only Jesus was able to do so, and now He wants to live His life through me in the power of the Holy Spirit.*

That statement embodied the essence of the truths which were unfolding for me. I called it the Grace/Faith understanding of the Christian life. It is G-R-A-C-E, **G**od's **R**iches **A**t **C**hrist's **E**xpense. It is a free gift that I neither merit nor earn. Thus, it is truly gospel, good news, gift, grace. It is faith because I believe what God declares, and I receive it as a gift. By appropriating it, I make it my own. It is expressed well in the words of the apostle Paul: "Blessed be the God and Father of our Lord Jesus Christ, who has blessed us in Christ with every spiritual blessing in the heavenly places" (Ephesians 1:3). In essence Paul is saying, "I praise you, Lord God, because you have bestowed on me all the spiritual riches Christ purchased for me. I thank you that all these blessings are mine in Christ Jesus. I believe you, and I thank you!"

A Scottish preacher expressed this profound truth concerning salvation and the Christian life in this way, of course speaking with his heavy Scottish accent:

> *God thought it.*
> *Christ bought it.*
> *The Holy Spirit wrought it.*
> *The Bible brought it.*
> *The devil fought it.*

But thank God, I got it!

Note, it is God's work from beginning to end. He planned it before the foundation of the world. Christ purchased every aspect of it through His atoning and sanctifying work. The Holy Spirit reveals it to the heart of the receptive. The Bible is the vehicle that carries this truth to us. The devil is arraigned against this complete redemption in Christ. And we need to receive this gift of salvation by faith as we give thanks to God and testify to it with our mouths.

My task as preacher and pastor is to present this good news in as clear and persuasive a manner as possible as the Spirit's instrument so that my hearers will understand and hearken to it in faith and surrender. This truth, when embraced, sets the captive free from bondage to self and legalism.

Church On Fire

Lord, Give Me North Heights, Or I Die
Chapter 9

"Ask of me, and I will make the nations your heritage, and the ends of the earth your possession." (Psalm 2:8)

He has shown his people the power of his works, in giving them the heritage of the nations. (Psalm 111:6)

The promise to Abraham and his descendants, that they should inherit the world, did not come through the law but through the righteousness of faith. (Romans 4:13)

John Knox, the great reformer in Scotland, prayed, "Lord, give me Scotland, or I die!" The Lord heard and answered his persistent prayers and used him as a mighty instrument for reformation and revival in that nation.

Motivated by Knox's example, I prayed, "Lord, give me North Heights, or I die!" I was praying for revival. Such a petition may sound strange to many, but it is biblical. As an example, many missionaries have departed for foreign lands asking the Lord to give them the nation to which they are being sent, that it be won for Christ. This petition is based on Psalm 2:8: "Ask of me, and I will make the nations your heritage, and the ends of the earth your possession."

Extending God's Kingdom on Earth

This messianic psalm clearly reflects God's redemptive plan for the world. The Father spoke this word to His Son, and our Lord

Jesus purchased salvation for all the nations on earth. The Lord redeemed us to be His instruments for bringing news of salvation to all peoples. He chose us to be His servants to reclaim the nations for His kingdom. In Romans 4:13, God promised Abraham and his heirs that they would inherit the world. All believers are Abraham's offspring, and thus heirs of the promise, as Paul makes clear in verse 16.

Thus the Lord commands us, as heirs to the promise, to claim for His kingdom those people and places that are in our sphere of influence and responsibility. And He calls us to lift up our eyes and see the vast territories beyond the horizon to ask for the lost souls in the ends of the earth. In other words, the Lord calls us to be His instruments to reclaim and regain enemy-occupied territory for His kingdom. This involves spiritual warfare, a battle in the spirit realm.

The enemy will resist our advances. But God has promised to give us the nations as our inheritance. His promises are unlimited from His perspective. They are limited only by our lack of faith, obedience, and perseverance. John Wesley offered an example when he said, "The world is my parish." He together with his brother Charles and George Whitfield became instruments in a great spiritual awakening that swept across England and brought major social reforms.

These truths were the basis for my prayer in 1962, "O Lord, give me North Heights or I die." First of all, this petition meant my own life needed to be under the Lordship of Jesus Christ in all areas. So, following this pattern, I prayed, "O Lord, give me myself or I die!"

Then I cried, "O Lord, give me my family or I die!" In this petition, I was claiming each family member for Christ and His headship.

The next area of responsibility was North Heights. "O Lord," I pleaded, "give me North Heights or I die!" This was a plea for Jesus' Lordship over the whole congregation.

Then, I did something I'm sure you have never done. I told the Lord what to do and how to do it! I prayed, "Lord, renew the whole church—not 10 percent, not 25 percent, not 50 percent, or even 75 percent, but 100 percent. And Lord, give me the whole church without split or division."

My request for the whole congregation to be renewed spiritually appeared impossible. But God specializes in the impossible. He is the God of the impossible: "For with God nothing will be impossible" (Luke 1:37). Furthermore, for the believer, nothing is impossible. Jesus declared, "For truly, I say to you, if you have faith as a grain of mustard seed, you will say to this mountain, 'Move from here to there,' and it will move; and *nothing will be impossible to you*" (Matthew 17:20, emphasis added).

I had no idea how the Lord would answer my request. Nevertheless, I made the request, and the Lord began the work of renewing one person after another, and one aspect of the congregation after another.

Often, I saw little or no visible evidence that the Lord was answering my prayer. But for the next decade, I kept repeating this petition daily, "O Lord, give me North Heights, or I die."

"Revival Will Be Coming to North Heights!"

I began praying for revival at the altar of the church every Monday evening. Soon, a few men who were experiencing spiritual renewal joined me in prayer. One man had participated in the outpouring of the Holy Spirit at another Lutheran church two years earlier. As he observed what was taking place at North Heights, he said, "Morris, you have revival going on here." We were experiencing revival, but only on a small scale at that time.

One Sunday morning in 1962, I declared in my sermon, "Revival will be coming to North Heights!" At the time, the spiritual awakening at North Heights was new and confined to a small number of people. It would take a mighty miracle for the whole church to be revived, I realized. I knew I was stepping way out on a limb in making such a prophetic proclamation. Yet, I spoke what I felt the Spirit told me to say. As I shook hands with parishioners after the service, a very dedicated spiritual member said to me, "That will never happen." She desired revival, but in looking at reality she felt it was impossible. She died without seeing it come into reality.

That Sunday afternoon, I went through self-condemnation over the radical pronouncement I had made. "How do you know revival will come? Look at the spiritual condition of the church. In earlier years a number of zealous Christians prayed earnestly for and witnessed ardently to unconverted members, but with little results. How can you say revival will come to North Heights? What if it doesn't? Then you will be seen as a false prophet." This was the argument going on in my mind.

Finally I said, "Lord, if I spoke falsely this morning, You will have to forgive me. I spoke what I felt You inspired me to say. I spoke it by faith. If people think I was crazy in what I said, so be it. But I am going to believe You for it." I left the matter there, and with that I took my Sunday afternoon nap.

Progress was slower than I had anticipated. Fewer members were seeking spiritual renewal than I desired. At the same time, I heard of significant numbers coming into renewal in other churches in other parts of the country. "Why not at North Heights?" I wondered. I was discouraged.

An Answer From God

One morning in my personal devotions, shortly after my prophetic proclamation in 1962, I asked the Lord why He had brought us back from Madagascar, since we had felt called to serve there as lifetime missionaries. We had been seeing tangible results in our mission work. So, why did He take us from such a promising place and put us in a seemingly barren field?

Suddenly the thought entered my mind, "You will find the answer in your Bible reading today." I was studying Isaiah in my devotions and had come to chapter 41. In my reading, the words I have highlighted in bold, jumped out at me:

> "**But you, Israel, my servant,**
> Jacob, **whom I have chosen,**
> The offspring of Abraham, my friend;
> **You whom I took from the ends of the earth,**
> **And called from its farthest corners,**
> **Saying to you, 'You are my servant,**
> **I have chosen you and not cast you off';**
> **Fear not, for I am with you,**
> **Be not dismayed, for I am your God;**

I will strengthen you, I will help you,
I will uphold you with my victorious right hand." (Isaiah
41:8-10, emphasis added)

I sensed that this was a personal word for me. It was so very specific. Madagascar, the large island off the southeast coast of Africa, is at the ends of the earth, its farthest corner. It's the end of the line. You don't go beyond there. The Lord assured me that He brought us back from our mission work on that far-off island, and that He had not cast us off, but had chosen us and would strengthen us.

I kept reading, but now with a heightened sense of expectancy:

> *"Behold, all who are incensed against you*
> *Shall be put to shame and confounded;*
> *Those who strive against you*
> *Shall be as nothing and shall perish.*
> *You shall seek those who contend with you,*
> *But you shall not find them;*
> *Those who war against you*
> *Shall be as nothing at all.*
> *For I, the Lord your God,*
> *Hold your right hand;*
> *It is I who say to you, 'Fear not,*
> *I will help you.'" (vv. 11-13).*

In regard to revival and my ministry in general, I was feeling a lack of support and a wait-and-see attitude from many in the congregation. In that context, these verses were further words of encouragement for me. I was strengthened by this passage again nine years later when a small but vocal group openly opposed me and my leadership in the charismatic renewal.

Rivers on Bare Heights

Prior to my experience of the filling with the Holy Spirit, I felt dry
in my spiritual life and often expressed my spiritual thirst in the
words of the Psalmist:

*As a hart longs for flowing streams,
So longs my soul for thee, O God.
My soul thirsts for God, for the living God.
When shall I come and behold the face of God? (Psalm
42:1-2)*

*O God, thou art my God, I seek thee,
My soul thirsts for thee;
My flesh faints for thee,
As in a dry and weary land where no water is. (Psalm 63:1)*

I was frustrated over my dry spiritual condition. Out of my thirst, I
began drinking of the living water of the Holy Spirit. Spiritual thirst
leads to the outpouring of living water. This living water is the
Holy Spirit being poured out. The thirst of my soul and my cry for
the Holy Spirit led to my spiritual awakening in the spring of 1962,
spoken of earlier.

My heart-cry and that of other spiritually thirsty souls at North
Heights was a precursor to renewal that would come to our
church. I saw this truth stated so beautifully in Isaiah 41. I felt that
it was divine confirmation of the prophetic message of the coming
revival to North Heights of which I had spoken that Sunday
morning in 1962:

*"When the poor and needy seek water,
And there is none,*

And their tongue is parched with thirst,
I the Lord will answer them,
I the God of Israel will not forsake them.
I will open rivers on the bare heights,
And fountains in the midst of the valleys;
I will make the wilderness a pool of water,
And the dry land springs of water.
I will put in the wilderness the cedar,
The acacia, the myrtle, and the olive;
I will set in the desert the cypress,
The plane and the pine together;
That men may see and know,
May consider and understand together,
That the hand of the Lord has done this,
The Holy One of Israel has created it." *(Isaiah 41:17-20, emphasis added)*

"The bare heights is North Heights!" This stood out—almost screamed out—to me. It was like the Lord speaking that He will open "rivers on the bare heights, on North Heights." It would not be a little stream and not just one little river, but rivers. He showed me that from North Heights would flow rivers in all directions. "Wow!" I said aloud.

I recognized that at their source, rivers may not appear like major waterways, but the further they flow from their origin, the larger they become. "So is that what will happen at North Heights?" I asked the Lord. He assured me that His Word is not void of power, that it will accomplish what He declares.

I had visited Itasca State Park in northern Minnesota in the early 1950s. Lake Itasca is the fountainhead of the mighty Mississippi River. At its origin, it is only a small stream a few feet wide.

Looking at that little flow of water, I had a hard time imagining that it would develop into a river that is the watershed for half of the United States. At the point at which it flows into the Gulf of Mexico, 1,200 miles later, it is a huge body of water two miles wide.

As I considered the rivers of living water that would flow from North Heights according to the Word of the Lord, I thought of the Mississippi River at its source. This is what we looked like at that time. Would North Heights really become a mighty river some day? I could not conceive it in my imagination. It certainly did not appear possible back in 1962.

His promise was for the poor and needy who earnestly seek the Spirit's outpouring. As I meditated on these verses, I had a hard time visualizing how this would become reality.

A Promised Outpouring

That dynamic 41st chapter of Isaiah whetted my appetite for more. I kept reading and finding gems of truth and marvelous personal promises in passage after passage. In chapter 44, the Lord gave further clear confirmation that He was going to pour His Spirit on us and revive us:

> *"For I will pour water on the thirsty land,*
> *And streams on the dry ground;*
> *I will pour my Spirit upon your descendants,*
> *And my blessing on your offspring.*
> *They shall spring up like grass amid waters,*
> *Like willows by flowing streams.*
> *This one will say, 'I am the Lord's,'*
> *Another will call himself by the name of Jacob,*

And another will write on his hand, 'The Lord's,'
And surname himself by the name of Israel." (Isaiah 44:3-5,
emphasis added)

This prophecy reaffirmed the promises in chapter 41. Perhaps this was what the Lord spoke to Amos: "Surely the Lord God does nothing, without revealing his secret to his servants the prophets.... The Lord God has spoken; who can but prophesy?" (Amos 3:7-8).

It was the Lord speaking through me that Sunday morning in 1962, prophesying that revival was to come to North Heights. Now, forty-six years later, I stand in amazement at the fulfillment of His word of promise.

At the time of my retirement from North Heights, I reflected on this, that we had been experiencing genuine revival at North Heights in fulfillment of these promises in Isaiah and in answer to prayer. The Lord had been pouring His Spirit on the poor and needy, on the thirsty and dry land—on the bare heights. Spiritual awakening had come to countless lives and into the whole church. It had been continuous revival over an extended period of years. The rivers were flowing from North Heights out to all continents. Numbers of thirsty souls have come from dozens of nations to drink from the living waters, and hundreds from our church have gone out across the globe to bring renewal fire to seekers after revival.

The focus of renewal at North Heights was on restoration of the biblical teaching on the Christian life—that is, who we are and what we have in Christ and the Holy Spirit's work of transforming believers into the image of Christ. This was not to the neglect of the gifts of the Spirit. While we emphasized who we are in Christ, we also stressed the mighty works He does through us. Who we are determines what we do.

At North Heights, we saw seasons of testing, and we witnessed times of vibrant life and mighty manifestations. Through the decades the Lord has graciously continued to pour out His Spirit on our congregation. For this we give Him all glory and thanks!

Church On Fire

The Spirit Is Poured Out On North Heights
Chapter 10

*"For I will pour water on the thirsty land,
and streams on the dry ground;
I will pour my Spirit upon your descendants,
and my blessing on your offspring." (Isaiah 44:3)*

My relationship with North Heights Lutheran Church began in 1961 when I was called as pastor. I was thrust into a situation in which the congregation faced major decisions, one of which had the potential of splitting the church, and I felt under intense pressure.

These pressures led me to surrender myself, my ministry, the church, and all its challenges over to the Lord. I recognized that I had not created the problems, nor could I resolve them. So I prayed, "Lord, this is your problem, not mine." I released them to Him and left them there.

Our Introduction to Charismatic Renewal

In the process of seeking a deeper relationship with the Lord and a greater dependency upon Him, I was introduced to charismatic renewal, a contemporary movement in which the church is being revived through the person, power, and gifts of the Holy Spirit. I searched Scripture to see if this phenomenon was true to the whole and heart of the Bible. I became convinced that the Holy Spirit's anointing and gifts were intended not only for the New Testament church, but are necessary for effective and fruitful ministry today as well. Thus, in early 1962 I sought the enduement with power from on high and the gifts of the Spirit.

Bonnie and I opened our home to fellowship gatherings, where we introduced many from across the Twin Cities to the outpouring of the Holy Spirit. North Heights members were more reticent in accepting the charismatic experience, although I refrained from using that term because of the prevalent teaching in many churches that this practice was confined to the New Testament age. Furthermore, I recognized that the members needed to gain confidence in me, and it takes time for a new pastor to be accepted. In the early stages of renewal at North Heights, those most open to the baptism of the Holy Spirit were those converted to Christ during my ministry. These were largely men in their late 20s and early 30s. They became zealous for the Lord and sought all the teaching they could get in their spiritual thirst.

During our first dozen years at North Heights, the confidence level of the members toward me and charismatic renewal grew significantly, and this led to the spiritual transformation of the congregation. My prayers for the renewal of the whole church without split or division were answered. My pastoral leadership was established and accepted. The Holy Spirit brought unity into a potentially divisive situation, and the unity was centered in Christ. As a result I had gained support from the members so as to be able to lead the church into a far expanded vision.

Freed by God's Grace

An important element of our spiritual renewal related to an understanding of the Christian life, witness, and ministry. The shift in my perception in these areas impacted the congregation significantly.

I knew that we are justified, or saved, by grace through faith, that this is God's work in Christ, and that we are to respond to the Holy Spirit's call by faith. But in regard to sanctification, or the ongoing Christian walk, I had a misperception that this was based on one's dedication and discipline. So I emphasized the need to be more zealous, to try harder. This led to performance orientation or legalism. But no amount of human effort proved sufficient. This approach resulted in introspection, self-condemnation, depression, and defeat.

After my charismatic experience in 1962, I discovered that the Christian life, like salvation, is 100 percent God's activity in Christ, and is to be received by faith and worked out in us by the Holy Spirit. Through His life, death, resurrection, and glorification Jesus fulfilled all that is required of us. Thus, God has blessed us in Christ with every spiritual blessing in the heavenly places. We need revelation of this truth and an appropriation of it in our hearts and lives. This is the grace/faith approach which frees us from the heavy burden of greater human willpower and more effort. Christian witness, service, and ministry are also God's work. As we are yielded and obedient instruments, the Holy Spirit will speak and work through us.

These biblical truths revolutionized my life, teachings, and ministry, and they transformed the congregation. They helped to shape North Heights into a grace-oriented community of faith.

At first I felt like it was speaking over the heads of the people. I received very little positive response. If I threw in a law sermon preaching against sin, telling the audience what not to do and what their duties and obligations were as believers, I received strong affirmation. I realized that we prefer having the law laid down on us, and the harder the better. But a steady diet of law leads to discouragement and depression. Eventually, one after another in the congregation came to understand and welcome the good news that God has done everything necessary for living the abundant Christian life, that He accomplished this in Christ, and now He wants to live this life in us by means of the Holy Spirit. Not only is Jesus our substitute in death, but He is also our substitute in life.

I introduced charismatic renewal and other associated changes into the congregation in an evolutionary manner rather than by revolutionary means. My vision and prayer was for the whole church to be renewed spiritually without division. By 1972 the whole direction of the church had become that of spiritual renewal.

A Christ-Centered Ministry

My style of ministry shifted from a traditional approach to a multitude and discipleship model patterned after Jesus. Christ ministered to the whole person in the love and power of the Holy Spirit. He had compassion on the people and healed them of their diseases. To the multitudes He spoke in parables and extended an invitation to follow Him. Those who forsook all and followed Him became His disciples. On various occasions Jesus withdrew with His disciples to teach and train them for ministry. Thus, He invested Himself in His disciples. They employed the same approach in their ministries.

Many younger couples were converted to Christ during this earlier period of my ministry, and they entered into the charismatic experience and discipleship training. They soon emerged into leadership roles in the church.

The Bethel Series, a two-year overview study of the Bible, became a major discipleship training program for us. I trained twelve teachers in an intensive course, and they in turn taught the materials in the congregational phase. Since the strength of the program is in the intensive portion, I chose to train one group after another in the highly disciplined program, and thus a number of highly committed, biblically knowledgeable leaders soon emerged.

The first pastors and missionaries to come out of North Heights were discipled in this manner. Out of this model a three-year congregational biblical survey program emerged in the early 1970s. This was followed in the mid-'70s with a School of the Bible. Many classes were offered and were advertised in the Twin Cities newspapers. North Heights became a teaching church reaching out into the region, but it was not with the intent of taking members away from other churches. If people asked me whether they should leave their church and join North Heights, I consistently encouraged them to stay and bloom where they were presently members.

In retrospect, I am not sure if that was always the right advice. I should have said that their primary responsibility is for their children. If the atmosphere was not conducive for their children's spiritual life and growth in their present setting, then they should go where they can flourish in their Christian life. I saw cases where the older children did not have a positive spiritual climate for their nurture, but then the family came to North Heights and the younger children came alive spiritually. In one such case, the mother, a college professor, regretted that they had not come earlier so the older children, now disinterested, could have had the opportunity to respond to Christ during their formative years in a positive spiritual environment.

Mentoring Young Members for Ministry

In earlier years I taught a Wednesday evening Bible study and led Friday night fellowships. I met with individuals and small groups for spiritual formation. Also, I took some newer converts with me to nursing homes and gospel missions, or on hospital visits and healing prayer sessions. Several became active in youth ministry, assisting me and our youth directors. They grew in their spiritual life and ministry through observation and participation.

Hundreds, even thousands, of life changing stories could be told, but let me share the experience of one couple. Merlin "Mork" Morken and his fiancée, Linda, sought a church where they could get married. Being new to the Twin Cities, they were not acquainted where to go, and so they opened the Yellow Pages to "Churches – Lutheran," closed their eyes, and put their fingers together on the page. Whichever church their fingers touched would be the one they would call. Their fingers pointed to North Heights!

Mork called and asked if I would perform their marriage service. I set up an appointment for them to meet with me. He was a Lutheran from northwestern Minnesota with many years of perfect Sunday school attendance. Linda was Catholic, growing up in a family that moved often and was destitute. From early childhood she had been told by her parents to steal food and other necessities wherever she could find them.

I shared Jesus with Mork and Linda, and they responded favorably to the extent of their understanding, but in retrospect my words went over their heads. I went ahead and performed the marriage service.

In the new members class that they soon attended, I explained the way of salvation as simply as possible. They expressed a measure of faith to the extent of their understanding, and they were accepted as members. A couple of years later Mork was elected to the Board of Deacons. They volunteered to be youth advisors. Around this same time they also came to me for marriage counseling.

It was on a youth group roller skating outing that a breakthrough began. As I skated around the rink with them, I asked how it was going in their marriage. They replied, "Better," but they still had problems. I invited them to attend a Friday night fellowship meeting at our home. I told them that they would meet other couples their age who were on fire for the Lord. They went and gave their hearts fully to the Lord and were filled with the Holy Spirit. There was new fire in their hearts and new smiles on their faces.

Mork and some other young men from North Heights befriended Paul Bakken, a new manager of a nearby Amoco station. They invited Paul and his wife to our church and to the home fellowships. The Bakkens responded and were introduced to spiritual realities they had never known existed.

Shortly afterward, Mork sensed that they were ready to accept Christ as Savior, but he did not know how to lead them. So he asked me to show him how to lead someone to faith in Christ. I wanted to demonstrate this to him, so Bonnie and I invited the

Bakkens and Morkens to our house for dinner. In the course of the conversation I asked Paul and his wife if they knew Jesus as their Savior. They weren't sure. I shared with them the story of salvation and how to respond. I asked if they were ready to give their lives to Jesus and receive Him into their hearts as Lord and Savior. They said yes. Then I led them in prayer of surrender, confession of sins, and acceptance of Jesus as Savior and Lord.

There was a double benefit: Paul and his wife came to personal living faith in Christ, while Mork and Linda saw how to lead others to Christ. The Bakkens now live in San Diego and are committed Christians and active leaders in their church. The Morkens have led a large number of individuals to faith in Christ in the forty years since that night in our home.

The very next year, 1969, Mork was instrumental in founding the North Heights Prison Ministry, which he has led to this day. Weekly meetings are held in the Stillwater State Prison chapel with a capacity audience. Double that number desire to attend but cannot due to the limited space, so only the first seventy to sign up are permitted. The meetings include vibrant worship, Bible studies, teachings, testimonies, prayers for needs of prisoners, and healings. Miracles are a vital aspect of the ministry. In the past thirty-nine years this ministry has impacted thousands of prisoners, many of whom have committed their lives to Christ and been filled with the Holy Spirit. A number have been healed through prayer and the laying on of hands. It is the largest ministry at the prison. The ministry owns and operates seven Christ-centered half-way houses for those released from prison, and reaches out to assist families of prisoners who face numerous difficulties.

Linda has been a teacher and in leadership in Women's Aglow Fellowship for years and served on the Council of Elders at North Heights. Both are popular speakers at churches, conferences, and retreats. They are bold and unashamed in their witness to the Lord Jesus Christ. As they pray, the Holy Spirit touches people in a powerful way.

As a result of their entrepreneurial spirit and hard work, Mork and Linda have built a large successful trucking business, which they operate under the Lordship of Jesus Christ. In the 1960s, when several others in our church felt God's call into pastoral ministry and missionary service, they felt left out. "Why is God not calling us into ministry?" they wondered. In effect, the Lord did call them into ministry and has used them in effective and fruitful service in His Kingdom through their business, church ministry, and prison and community outreach. This is just one example of fruit being produced from discipleship ministry.

Following the Perfect Model

Early in my ministry at North Heights I sought to evaluate the fruitfulness of my endeavors. I found that much of my time was spent trying to resolve crisis situations among various parishioners. These cases required immediate response. I became the "ER" physician for relational and spiritual issues, dealing often with repeat cases of crises. "Where is the progress in their lives?" I asked myself. I was treating symptoms that kept cropping up. My efforts at dealing with root issues failed. The focus of these individuals was on the problem, and it appeared their eyes were closed to any deeper spiritual need. I noted that during their emergency some would attend church services, but when the difficulty eased up, they were nowhere to be seen until the next critical situation erupted. Some I never did see in church. I pondered, "Where is the fruit of this crisis ministry?"

I did not disparage meeting people in their time of need. I loved the people. I gave them all the time they needed. I came to know some very well, and enjoyed being with them. For those going through serious difficulties, it was a critical time. I did not want to minimize that. And I sought to penetrate to root issues, but usually met with limited success. The present crisis, or symptom, was uppermost on their agenda, and that needed to be attended to right away.

"Is there a better way?" I pondered. My thoughts were turned to a ministry model found in the New Testament. One person, the Lord Jesus Christ, stood out. He had a dual focus, ministry to multitudes and to disciples. He was unusually successful. I noted in His ministry to multitudes that He had a special burden for those who were hurting and rejected. He ministered in the full power of the Holy Spirit as He healed the sick and delivered the demonized, setting them free from every form of bondage (Acts 10:38). This He did out of deep compassion for them. He extended the invitation to the masses, "Come and follow Me." Those who forsook all and came to Him He called disciples.

Then I noticed that at various times He withdrew from the crowds to be alone with His disciples. I observed that He had different levels of disciples: the one whom He loved, the three and four He took with Him on special occasions, the twelve whom He later called "Apostles," the seventy or seventy-two others whom He sent out two-by-two to announce His coming and to do the same works He did, and then the one hundred twenty gathered in the upper room after His resurrection. There were numerous other followers as well, also identified as disciples. To the inner core He gave special instruction and revealed truths hidden from the multitudes.

He addressed the twelve: "To you it has been given to know the secrets of the kingdom of heaven, but to them it has not been given…. But blessed are your eyes, for they see, and your ears, for they hear. Truly, I say to you, many prophets and righteous men longed to see what you see, and did not see it, and to hear what you hear, and did not hear it." (Matthew 13: 11, 16-17)

I recognized my need to function in similar style to that of my Master. But how? I found a way to do this in a more formal manner. It was a two-year intensive study program to gain an overview of the Bible. The initial phase was for the pastor to train a dozen or so highly committed persons who in turn would teach the Bible to others on the congregational phase. This highly effective course was called the *Bethel Series*. It was developed by Pastor Harley Swiggum and was being widely utilized in churches at the time I was pursuing the discipleship training direction. The teacher training program required a commitment by participants of ten to twelve hours weekly in study and class session.

Jim Schwartz, a recent convert, was eager for our church to get involved. He wanted to be part of it himself, so he volunteered to raise the money necessary, and he became the first one to sign up. So in the mid 1960s we launched the *Bethel Series* and entered into an intentional discipleship training direction. Not all members were pleased that I invested this amount of time with just a handful of persons. Some brought up the old adage that a pastor was not to have close friends in the congregation, but was to have equal relationship with all the constituents. However, when the skeptics began to see the positive fruit from the discipling ministry, they were no longer critical of it.

I had no trouble finding eager people to select for the program. Some were new converts, while others had been committed Christians all their lives. In addition to the excellent written materials and memorization accompanying the program, I added other basic teachings as part of the discipleship training. For some who had been long-term believers it meant unlearning some things they had believed in the past, principally a legalistic understanding of the gospel. For new believers who had little previous biblical knowledge, it was one new discovery after another. It was eye-opening for them. They embraced the teaching as a sponge absorbs water. I said publicly that I would put any member of this group up to any seminarian in terms of knowledge of the Bible.

As we entered the second year of the teacher training phase, several in the class felt the Lord's calling to be missionaries, pastors, and evangelists—callings they pursued after completing the course. I said to the Lord, "These are the people I thought would be the instruments in renewing North Heights, and here you are taking them away." Then I sensed the Lord saying, "The first fruits belong to me." And so I released them to the Lord and to His calling on their lives.

Half of the class members felt called to remain and be part of the renewal of the congregation. They became teachers of the *Bethel Series* to scores of members during the next two years in the congregation phase. This program became a major step in raising the biblical literacy of the parishioners and of firming up the biblical and spiritual foundation of the congregational life and ministry.

After the completion of the initial teacher training phase, I wondered "Where are we to go from here?" I reflected on the petition I had been praying, "Lord, give me North Heights or I die!" Some on whom I had relied to be key persons in the renewal of the church felt called into other ministries. Now what was I to do? For a whole year I lost the vision of the church being completely renewed spiritually. It seemed impossible to me. I continued doing the ministry that needed to be done, but this with the vision dead and buried. If it was to be fulfilled, the Lord would have to bring it into reality.

Harley Swiggum, the developer of the *Bethel Series*, met with pastors involved in the program in Minneapolis that summer. He explained that the strength of the program was in the teacher training phase. He encouraged us to start another class utilizing the same program as that found in the teacher training one, but call it "An Intensive Bible Overview Class." That struck a chord with me. I enlisted another dozen highly enthused participants.

This group was deeply committed to the Lord. They were serious in pursuing a fuller knowledge of the Bible. As with the initial class, I did expository study of the biblical texts and stories we were studying, and I brought in other teachings on the victorious Christian life. They became a close knit group and were eager to learn and grow. Little did I realize that this group would play an important role in the spiritual renewal of the whole congregation.

Reigniting the Vision

During the year of the lost vision, I sought other directions for my life and ministry. I knew that as a charismatic I would not receive any calls from other churches to serve as pastor. I visited seminaries where I could pursue a doctoral degree in missions or ministry, but I eliminated this possibility. How would I be able to support my family for the years it takes to get a doctor's degree? I did continue my studies toward a master of theology degree at Luther Seminary in St. Paul, which I completed in 1970. I did this in my spare time over and above my 60 to 75 hours a week in fulfilling my pastoral duties. All other doors seemed closed.

One day I received a flier in the mail announcing the U.S. Congress on Evangelism. It was to be held in the Minneapolis Auditorium in September 1969. I had the strong impression that I was to attend. But I noticed the registration fee was $75, which was a larger sum than I had. And with the church's very tight finances, would the trustees approve such a huge expenditure? They might feel it would break the bank. I felt the Lord telling me to go to this conference, and to simply submit the bill to the treasurer to pay, and not ask permission. It's easier to ask for pardon than for permission. I followed the inner direction I received, and this conference became one of the most significant events in my life.

Evangelist Billy Graham and *Lutheran Hour* speaker Oswald (Ozzie) Hoffman were co-chairmen. The messages were excellent. The need for the Holy Spirit's power and direction rang clear throughout the event. I sought the Spirit's guidance as to which workshops to attend. I felt led to go to one conducted by Garden Grove Community Church in Garden Grove, California. It was led by Harold Leetsma, co-pastor of the church. As he and his team shared what was taking place in their church and how it was happening, the vision for spiritual renewal of North Heights was ignited in me again.

I left the Congress with revived vision and fresh enthusiasm for renewal of the whole congregation. Those in the second *Bethel*

Series class caught it from me, and they became instruments in praying the renewal into being.

During 1962-71, the decade in which the foundation for renewal was being laid, membership grew from 562 to 1,280, a 128 percent increase. My father, the Rev. Morris G. C. Vaagenes, Sr., played an important part in this growth. He served part-time as visitation pastor from 1963 to 1969, and as such made hundreds of calls to new residents, visitors, and those in the community who did not belong to a church. He was instrumental in bringing in many new members.

Charismatic renewal was introduced into North Heights in 1962. In 1972 the full direction of the church became that of renewal. This transformation took place totally from within the church without any one with charismatic experience coming from other churches. A spirit of love and unity prevailed. The presence of the Holy Spirit was evident in the worship services and activities. This was truly the Lord's doing and to Him belongs all credit and glory.

Revival Among the Youth

A key element of the spiritual renewal of the whole congregation was the revival that took place among the youth. I had not introduced the youth to the outpouring of the Holy Spirit and the spiritual gifts for fear it would get back to the parents, and some might be disturbed. But this changed in 1971 when we called Steve Woita, a Luther Seminary student, to serve as youth director. He had been active in a dynamic ministry on college campuses called Lutheran Youth Encounter (LYE), and he brought LYE teams to minister at our youth retreats. These teams introduced our junior and senior high youth to the Spirit-filled life and to the gifts of the Spirit. Their worship, teaching, buoyant spirit, and fire for the Lord touched the hearts of many young people, and large numbers responded. On one weekend retreat, during which the teaching was on the outpouring of the Spirit, the youth came to the altar one group after another to receive the baptism with the Holy Spirit. I prayed for at least three dozen youth who sought the filling with the Holy Spirit.

A powerful revival broke out among our young people, and this spread to their parents and into their schools. Woita started a youth singing group called "His Gang." The young people had a zeal for the Lord. They gathered at the altar every evening to pray, sing, study the Bible, and lead others to Christ. They were vibrant witnesses in their school and wherever they went. They witnessed to young people in the Rosedale Mall and led them to the Lord. They carried their Bibles with them to classes and activities. They were unashamed of witnessing of salvation in Christ. The revival among the youth became a major catalyst leading to the spiritual renewal of the church.

At our summer Bible camp I offered to teach an optional course on spiritual warfare during a free time for the campers. While attendance was optional, literally everyone attended, and the young people ate up the teaching. One month, later just before the start of school, Randy Schmidt, a leader among the youth and a goalie on the school's high ranked hockey team, came to me to get refreshed on the Bible passages I taught.

Then on Labor Day, some fifty of our youth on their own initiative marched around Kellogg High School seven times taking authority over the spiritual forces of evil in the students and school and declaring Jesus as Lord over the school. They were following the pattern given in Joshua 1:3, "Every place that the sole of your foot will tread upon I have given to you, as I promised to Moses." The atmosphere in the school was different that year. Some months later "His Gang" sang at the school's talent program. In introducing their songs Randy started preaching, and he received a positive response from the students.

Not everyone at North Heights was pleased with the revival taking place in our church. In early 1972 a few members objected to the church's spiritual emphasis and charismatic renewal. They sought endorsement for their cause from our denominational headquarters but failed to gain any support. They did find some empathy from a professor at Luther Seminary, who later apologized to me for giving support to those seeking to cause division. They also tried to get backing from other North Heights members, but found few sympathizers, and so they left peacefully for other churches. The atmosphere was tense for a time, but after they withdrew, peace settled over the church, and soon the direction of the whole church became that of spiritual renewal. Relations with those who left have been good. I hold nothing against them or anyone else who has opposed me or the direction I sought to lead.

In 1972 contemporary praise choruses and scripture songs were introduced into the Sunday morning worship service, while retaining many of the traditional elements. The changes were a blend of the new and the old, and they were accompanied with biblical teaching on worship. After worshiping in the new style for a few months, the congregation was polled regarding response to the changes. Every response was very positive and supportive of the new style of worship. There was not one objection. Worship had taken on fresh meaning. This new form of worship was a major factor in the renewal of the whole church.

Church On Fire

The Church Multiplies
Chapter 11

So the church ... had peace and was built up;
and walking in the fear of the Lord and in the comfort
of the Holy Spirit it was multiplied. (Acts 9:31)

In early 1972 I attended the Robert H. Schuller Institute on Successful Church Leadership at Garden Grove Community Church in Garden Grove, California. Only then did I realize that the workshop that had impacted me so powerfully at the U.S. Congress on Evangelism was conducted by the congregation Robert Schuller served, now known as the Crystal Cathedral.

"I Had a Vision on the Twelfth Floor"

My horizons were greatly expanded and my vision significantly enlarged at the Institute. Dr. Schuller had the gift of inspiring vision and of dreaming dreams in his listeners. My life and ministry were forever transformed at this Institute. I had a vision on the 12th floor of the Tower of Hope. I was in Dr. Schuller's office, and from that vantage point I could see the surrounding community in all directions. I felt that North Heights' neighborhood was more conducive for drawing people to the church. Yet this church was several times larger than the one I was serving.

I asked how they were able to attract so many. "Every person within a 20 to 30 minute driving range who does not go to church is our mission field," was the answer given me. Dr. Schuller said in one of his presentations that they could not stop growing as long as there were unchurched and unsaved people in their area.

The vision I received was that our primary, immediate harvest field would be those living within 15 to 20 minutes driving range of our church. With so many Lutheran churches in the Twin Cities area, parish boundaries were established for new congregations in newly developed suburbs. These were guidelines and not a restrictive rule. Yet for the sake of good relationships with neighboring churches, I sought to abide by these borders. We limited our outreach to these boundaries.

But at the Institute these blinders came off, and now the whole region became our mission field. It was as with Jesus by the village well in Samaria. In a conversation with a woman who came to the well, Jesus offered her living water. Her spiritual thirst was stirred up. She had met the Messiah, and she rushed into town to tell everybody about her discovery. The townspeople came out to meet Jesus.

The disciples were oblivious to what was transpiring, and Jesus told them, "Do you not say, 'There are yet four months, then comes the harvest'? I tell you, lift up your eyes, and see how the fields are already white for harvest" (John 4:35). He was seeking to open their eyes to see even the Samaritans as a harvest field for the Kingdom of God.

At this Institute I also began to envision North Heights as a faith-filled community with a positive environment in which Spirit-inspired visions and dreams would be nourished and would flourish.

On my first Sunday back in the pulpit I preached a sermon entitled, "I Had a Vision on the Twelfth Floor." I shared my experience in Dr. Schuller's office. It was my declaration of a vastly enlarged vision for the congregation. The blinders were off. "Anyone within a fifteen minute driving range who does not know Christ as Savior and Lord is our mission field," I declared. "We cannot stop growing while there are unsaved souls in our vicinity."

Nothing Less Than Excellence

It was I who needed to be set free from a limited view for the congregation. I had to get freed from a small vision. The conviction became established in my heart that our church must grow and never stop growing, not for the sake of bigness but for the ingathering of people into the kingdom. Our church needed to be on fire for the Lord so as to attract those seeking genuine spiritual life. "The more we are aglow with the Spirit, the more people will be attracted to our church and ultimately to the Lord," I expressed.

I was not willing to settle for a medium-sized church. I added, "A spiritually live church, by virtue of its zeal for the Lord and for the lost, will grow. That is natural cause and effect. This means that North Heights will become a large church." I don't especially care for the term mega-church, but I knew that this is what a dynamic, spiritually on-fire church would become. I was not willing to settle for anything less than excellence.

The matter was settled in my heart. The church, empowered by the Spirit, would multiply. That's the very nature of the Holy Spirit. His vision is for the entire world to hear the good news that Jesus Christ died to make atonement for the whole lost human race, and His mission is to bring conviction of sin and to draw all to salvation in Christ. That is the Spirit at work in our church. We cannot settle for anything less than what the Spirit yearns for.

We weren't geared for explosive growth. We needed a complete paradigm shift. We could not continue to operate simply under human wisdom and then ask the Lord to bless it. We had it turned around. We needed to start with His will. What does He want us to do? And how does He want us to accomplish his will?

This meant that we must examine what we were doing, and find out if this was His will for us. And we needed to examine how we were doing the work to see if this was the way He wanted us to operate.

Rethinking Christian Education

The existing programs and ministries were put through a renewal process in the early 1970s, and many new ones were birthed. We raised the question with each ministry, "What does the Holy Spirit want to do through us and how does He desire to do it? What are the needs He wants us to meet?" We searched the Scriptures for principles, patterns, and practices to guide us. And we sought the Spirit's guidance for direction. No longer were we satisfied with doing church as usual because that's the way we always did it, or because this is the way other churches do it, or because our denomination suggests this is how to do programming.

The first area we examined was Christian Education. We asked the following questions and came to these conclusions:

1. *What is the goal of Christian education?* It is to lead people to maturity in Christ (Ephesians 4:11-16).

2. *Is the task of leading people to maturity completed at Confirmation?* No, it is a lifelong process, from cradle to grave.

3. *Where does the primary responsibility for the spiritual nurture of children belong—with the church or with parents?* Scripture is clear that the major role for training children lies with the parents. Thus, as a church we have a responsibility of aiding and equipping parents in the fulfilling of their obligation.

4. *What then is the church's role in relation with the spiritual nurture of children?* The church's function is not substitutionary to that of parents, but is secondary to, supportive of, and supplementary to their part.

We observed that children tend to adopt the faith of their parents, whether that faith is in Christ or in living a good life. One bases salvation on Christ's atoning sacrifice and righteousness, and the other on one's own good intentions and self-righteousness.

Since the primary responsibility for a child's welfare lies with the parents, we recognized that we needed to strengthen our adult program so as to equip parents to fulfill their vital role. This training was to include leading parents into assurance of salvation through Christ and spiritual growth in Him. We stressed that as a church we are partners with parents in the spiritual nurture of their children, but that the primary role belongs to them. In our children's ministries we enter into partnership with parents, and in our confirmation program we engage in a three-way partnership agreement signed by the parents, the church, and the confirmands.

Bible verse memorization is an important part of the Sunday school program. A fund in memory of Jason Wilkman provides incentive for memorizing Bible verses. Jason, son of David and Sandy Wilkman, was kidnapped and murdered in 1980 at the age of six. He was a wonderful boy who loved Jesus. His parents were leaders in the children's ministry. The Jason Wilkman Fund was established by his parents to encourage children to memorize Bible verses. Through the years thousands of dollars have been given to the fund, and God's Word has been inscribed in the hearts of thousands of children.

So many caring people have invested their lives into the children through the years that it would be impossible to name them all here. Their names and deeds are written in God's heavenly record.

Our Christian Education department sponsored a Sunday school during the founding years of the Hmong Lutheran Church near the State Capitol. For twenty years we have conducted a Sunday school and Vacation Bible School for Native American children at Little Earth of United Tribes in Minneapolis. Gail Baez, senior attorney for Hennepin County, has given leadership to this outreach. Other children's ministries included Hand in Hand led by Michelle Thompson. Many additional creative activities were conducted including assisting other churches in their children's ministries.

Spirit-Anointed Music Ministry

The music ministry went through transformation also. Senior choirs are a staple in church life. Yet it was a continuous struggle to get enough choir members. Every effort to recruit more singers failed. Due to budget restrictions in earlier years, choir directors were often unpaid volunteers.

One year in the mid 1960s, the volunteer director and the choir members had difficulty coordinating their schedules for rehearsal. The result was that we had no choir for several months. Then in early February I sought to resurrect the choir for Lent and Easter, and decided I would direct it myself. I announced short rehearsals for Wednesday evenings at 6:30 just before the 7 O'clock Lenten services.

But my effort was no more successful than before. Nevertheless we managed to sing at each Lenten service and Sunday morning worship service. Our last Sunday for the season was Confirmation Day in mid-May. As director I chose one of my favorite anthems, "How Lovely Is Thy Dwelling Place" from Johannes Brahms' *German Requiem*.

Following our finale, the Holy Spirit showed me that I was trying to do the work instead of letting the Lord do it, whether through me or whomever he chose. I remembered the theme verse of my ministry, "Unless the Lord builds the house, those who build it labor in vain" (Psalm 127:1).

My efforts were limited, and the work was burdensome. So I said, "Lord, I quit." I thought I heard "Good" coming from heaven. I said, "Lord, I will let the choir die. If you want me to conduct a funeral service and burial for the choir, I will do it." Then it dawned on me that our last anthem was taken from a *Requiem*, or funeral mass. We sang at our own funeral and didn't realize it. I added, "I will not direct or sing in the choir or play the organ any more. If you want a choir, you will have to raise it up and you will need to find a director."

The following Saturday morning Mark Shepperd, our skilled organist, came to church to practice. I shared this story with him.

Mark said, "That's funny. Recently I felt that the Lord wanted me to be minister of music here, but I didn't know how to approach you". I lifted up a quick prayer: "Lord, is Mark the one you have chosen?" I sensed an affirmative response. I told Mark the job was his.

A few minutes later Diana Isenhower Hanson came to rehearse with Mark. She was an excellent soloist who on occasion sang in our church. Both Mark and Diana were experiencing spiritual renewal in their lives. I told Diana of my experience. She replied, "That's strange. Twice this week I had dreams in which I saw myself involved in the start of a music ministry, and in both cases the church I saw was yours." I concluded that the Lord had chosen her to come to North Heights and to assist Mark.

Over the course of the summer many obstacles arose which made it appear that Mark and Diana would not be able to direct the music ministry. But this is typical of how visions come into reality. At some point it appears impossible of being fulfilled, and necessitates persevering prayer and faith. In this case the difficulties were overcome.

This time it was the Lord who was to resurrect the choir. Mark and Diana sought His plan and began praying it into reality. Mark felt led to pray for 40 choir members, double the previous number. Announcement was made inviting people to pray about singing in the choir. At the first rehearsal Mark counted the number present. There were 39. He was not going to start because the Lord had indicated 40. So they prayed, asking God for the 40th person to come. As they were praying, they heard the door squeak open, and they turned their heads to see who was coming in. It was Mike Sculley trying to sneak in quietly. The choir members could not help but break out into laughter at seeing the answer to their prayers. Mike, a husky self-conscious twenty-year-old young man, must have thought they were laughing at him. They were rejoicing in the Lord.

A New Direction in Worship

Thus, a whole new way of doing ministry and programming was being learned by the church. This affected not only the music ministry, but the worship life of the congregation as well. We became conscious that the object of our worship and music was God, and that we needed to be intentionally focused on Him. The hymns and worship songs were in effect making melody to Him. We were singing His praises for his Word and mighty actions. They were expressions of worship and adoration for who He is.

The choir no longer performed for the congregation. Instead, choir members were worshiping the Lord and leading the congregation in worship from their hearts. It became Spirit-inspired worship, of which Jesus spoke, "God is Spirit, and only by the power of his Spirit can people worship him as he really is" (John 4:24, TEV). This understanding brought a major revolution to the church's worship life.

Christ's Lordship over Finances

The two last areas to experience transformation were in finances and government. It was easier to continue doing the familiar than to launch out into the way of faith—that is, to move from the visible to the invisible. Paul writes that "we look not to the things that are seen but to the things that are unseen; for the things that are seen are transient, but the things that are unseen are eternal" (2 Corinthians 4:18). Later he writes that "we walk by faith, not by sight" (2 Corinthians 5:7). It is easier to trust in the known visible, tangible things than the invisible promises of God.

The pledge system and traditional stewardship programs had proven largely ineffective in motivating giving beyond that which provided a bare subsistence level for operations. The Stewardship Committee did its best through a variety of programs to bring in more funds for the Lord's work, but the results were always disappointing. Guilt motivation did not work, nor did pressure. We found that pledges made under pressure had to be collected with pressure.

It appeared that members responded in what could be called *reason giving*, that which depends on human calculation in determining the amount to give based on what one can afford. Sacrifice was encouraged—that is, give until it hurts. But giving in that manner is not happy giving.

The alternative is *revelation giving*, which is not on the basis of the visible resources but as the Spirit leads. It is giving based on God's invisible resources and not on one's limited human visible resources. But this type of giving does not come naturally. Martin Luther said that every person needs two conversions—one of the heart and the other of the pocketbook.

In 1972 I proposed that we shift from the ineffective traditional pledge system to a faith-challenge approach based on the *revelation giving* approach. This would involve abolishing pledges, the stewardship committee, a stewardship program, and all pleas and updates to the members. Instead of establishing the budget on the basis of pledges and projected income, we would ask each department to seek the Lord's will for their next year's program, submit these totals as the faith budget, and then pray in this amount. The trustees were not to make any cuts on the submitted requests. If the Lord was leading the department personnel in what He wanted them to do, and if He revealed a cost figure, then the trustees were not to second-guess those in charge of the proposed ministry. The task of the leaders and members was to pray this amount in and to trust the Lord to provide. The Lord would be our Source. The congregational members would be the means the Lord utilized to provide support. The faith principle is this: What the Lord ordered, we would trust Him to provide.

We studied the lives of such inspiring visionaries as George Mueller, Hudson Taylor, C.T. Studd, Norman Grubb, Rees Howells, and the Sisters of Mary, a Lutheran order in Darmstadt, Germany. These were all mighty in prayer, giants in faith, and abundantly fruitful in ministry. They became our models for faith finances. They made their personal and ministry needs known only to God in prayer, and then they trusted God to move the hearts of those He chose to supply the resources. Mighty miracles happened in every case. They and their ministries never lacked, although at times they were put to severe tests. Our faith grew through examining the many fantastic faith promises in the Scriptures and through reading the examples of those who had complete trust in the Lord to fulfill what He said He would do.

The first time I recommended the faith approach to the council, I was "shot out of the saddle," as Russ Schmidt, chairman of the council, put it. Council members learned that if they rejected actions I felt the Lord was directing for us, I would bring them up again at a later time. I learned that the first time a new idea was proposed, the normal reaction would often be to reject it. The negative reaction usually got voiced first, and often that opinion prevailed. I found that before making a decision on a new direction or proposal, I needed to take it into my inner being, yield it to the Lord in prayer, sleep on it, and listen to the Lord's still small voice, and then be ready to act on it no matter how impossible it may appear. The heart is to be trusted above the head.

The next year, the fall of 1973, I presented the proposal again to step out in faith in our church's finances, and it was approved. The chairman of the Board of Trustees, Leonard Ohlsson, resigned from the trustee board so he could lead a group every Monday evening to pray in the funds.

The last year under the old system the income decreased $2,000 from the previous year. I feel that this was likely due to the rejection of the faith approach. In 1974, the first year under the faith approach, the challenge budget was increased from $81,000 the previous year to $95,000. The weekly renewal prayer group prayed specifically for the $95,000 amount to come in. What were the results? Contributions jumped dramatically from $79,000 to $105,000, a 33 percent growth.

God's faithfulness continued throughout the years:

- In 1975 the faith budget figure was $125,000. Regular offerings were $131,000 with an additional $37,000 for the building fund, for a total of $165,000—a 60 percent increase over the previous year.

- The 1976 budget was $191,000, with regular income being $204,000, plus building fund giving of $38,000 for a total of $242,000—a 44 percent growth.

- In 1977 the faith budget was $320,000 and contributions were $323,000, a 33 percent jump.

- In 1978 the challenge budget was $517,000, with $500,000 contributed, for a hefty 55 percent increase.

- The budget for 1979 was set at $632,000. Regular income was $653,000, and building fund giving was $115,000, for a total of $768,000—a 52 percent growth.

- By 1987 total income had risen to $3,140,000, a miraculous 3,975 percent increase in fourteen years since moving to the faith approach!

The congregation shifted from some aspects of the faith finances in 1984 as it entered into the Lift Up Your Eyes capital fund drive for building a new facility at the Arden Hills campus to house a large sanctuary seating 1,500, classrooms and offices. Pledges were sought for the building program and bonds were sold for the portion not covered by pledges. The remaining indebtedness on the school building was incorporated into the pledge and bond figure.

There was anguish on the part of a number who had seen the blessings of the "no pledge" approach, but in the end the pledge/bond route for construction of the new Sanctuary was taken.

In one sense, the aspects of the faith finance approach that remains to the present is the "no pledge" for the regular budget and no stewardship programs. Another fund drive, Catch The Vision, was conducted in the mid 90s for building a very large

Family Life Center. Receipts for the fiscal year, 1996-97, came in at $6,500,000 including Catch The Vision giving. That is an astounding 8,228% growth in income in 24 years. To God belongs the glory! The total income for the financial year ending May 31, 2007, was $9,745,000.

The focus, however, was not on money, but on the Lordship of Jesus over finances. Individuals and families were challenged by the Holy Spirit to turn control of their finances to the Lord. Many did so, and applied these truths in their family finances and work situation, just as the church had given financial control to the Lord. This became a means for major spiritual growth. I believe that there was a direct link between the spiritual awakening in our church and the launching of the faith walk in finances.

Times of Testing, New Steps of Faith

This story would be incomplete without indicating that we have been tested in this faith walk on numerous occasions. Every new venture of faith leads to a new test. The challenge to take a step of faith so as to meet a drastic need has always come when our finances have been at a low point. "How much will it cost?" is the first question raised. And the second response is, "We cannot afford to do it." Instead we ought to ask, "Is this from the Lord? And if so, will we follow the guidance we have received? Will we trust the Lord to supply the funds? Will we pray in the funds?"

These are issues we have confronted at the launching of every new ministry or program. The issue is the Lordship of Jesus. It is a battle of faith. We discover that every new challenge from the Lord is larger than the previous one. By the Holy Spirit's enablement we have repeatedly overcome fear and stepped out in faith, although many times it has been a weak or faltering faith.

But we have found the Lord faithful again and again. To Him belongs the praise!

At the same time, we observe that our faith is tested through financial shortfalls. Every work of God must go through the fire. The Lord purges the work and His people as a means of purifying, cleansing, and correcting us so that we may serve Him in a right manner and spirit. He prunes the branches so that they may produce more fruit. Some of our tests have led to strengthening in our faith and purifying in our lives. The results, for good or ill, are based on our response. Through testing, our extremity becomes God's opportunity.

The Bible states that the love of money is the root of all evils (1 Timothy 6:10). This is a major area in which the Holy Spirit confronts us in our sanctification. Surrendering ownership of one's possessions to the Lord is a vital aspect of becoming a mature Christian. How can a servant of the Lord be entrusted with true spiritual riches if proved unfaithful in financial matters! Releasing one's finances to the Lord leads to peace and trust as well as freedom from bondage in money matters. It is an entrance into blessings untold. This is the way of living according to the promises of God and learning obedience to His voice in richer ways.

The North Heights congregation has been generous in support of the Lord's work whether at home or abroad. This is truly a miracle story. No appeals were made to the congregation, only to God. There were no gimmicks, no manipulation, no appeal to greed, and no heavy-handed law.

Numerous ministries were started during this time because of adequate income. The results were far beyond my expectations.

Church On Fire

The council and congregation experienced a tremendous boost in faith and in the power of prayer. We saw what can happen when we allow God to control our finances, and we learned to trust Him to fulfill His promises. His resources and provisions are unlimited.

Expansion, Growth and Fruitfulness
Chapter 12

So the word of the Lord grew and
prevailed mightily. Acts 19:20

With the large influx of new members and the generous increase in income, new programs were instituted and new staff members were called. Dick Denny, a former businessman, served as Lay Assistant Pastor from 1973 to 1976. Dick and Betty Denny's son Rick was killed in battle in the Viet Nam War. This drastically changed their lives. They were transformed from simply "pew warmer" Christians, as they had identified themselves, to committed Spirit-filled believers. Dick prayed that if the Lord would sell his business, he would serve Him in full-time ministry without pay. Within two weeks his company was sold. He served as business manager for Lutheran Youth Encounter and then at North Heights for three years, both without compensation and both with very fruitful ministry.

Added to the pastoral staff during my tenure were Rev. Alvin H. Rogen in 1970; Rev. Robert Burmeister and Rev. Erwin Prange in 1976; Rev. Milton Markworth and Dr. William Backus in 1977; Dr. W. Dennis Pederson in 1978; Dr. Byron Schmid in 1979; Rev. Larry Christenson and Rev. Randy Hansen in 1981; Dr. Greg Berglund, Rev. Bob Cottingham, and Rev. David Jore in 1982; Dr. Jeff Dorman in 1987; Rev. Steven Wiese in 1989; Dr. Carl Vaagenes in 1994; Dr. Allen Swanson in 1995; Rev. Dick Erickson in 1997; Dr. Mark Herringshaw in 1998; and Rev Eric Bluhm in 1999.

Church On Fire

A host of others were called to the program staff. Besides those already mentioned others who directed various ministries during my time of ministry included Joe Rickenback, Noreen Rickenback, Wesley Wheatley, Arlo Lien, Dennis Underwood, Pat Ose, Orlando Logelin, Haakon Oksnevad, Jean Beardon, Muriel Jensen, Jean Osell, Jon Ulrich, and a host of others. Valerie Johnson Peterson served as the first full-time parish secretary. Nap and Artis Bruneau served faithfully over a quarter century as directors of custodial services and housekeeping at the Roseville campus.

One person who deserves special mention is Janet Otto, who began volunteering at North Heights in 1957 and more than fifty years later is still donating her services. Janet maintains the membership rolls, addresses, and other data, and has seen the congregation grow from 250 members to more than 7,000 during this half century. Her mother volunteered with her in the early years, and now her daughter Anita is on children's ministry staff.

With a large full and part-time staff of 200 persons, it would be impossible to name all who served so faithfully. Deep gratitude is expressed to all staff members and to the huge number of volunteers who gave so generously of their time, talents, and treasures for the work of God's Kingdom, as well as all the faithful members who interceded, sacrificed and gave so generously.

When I came to North Heights, there were two boards: Deacons that had oversight for the spiritual life and programs, and Trustees that oversaw the finances and buildings. The nine members of each board and the chairman and secretary of the congregation comprised the church council. As the church grew, I sought to elevate the roles of the three committees, Christian education, youth and stewardship, by raising them to board status and to membership on the council. This was accomplished with council and congregation approval. This led to a council of forty-seven members.

In retrospect I noted the wisdom of this action in that I proposed a number of changes. These were brought to the respective board for action, and with their approval they were presented to the full council for discussion and decision. With input and approval by this large number of key members, the recommendations were refined in the process, many felt ownership of the decision and the changes were readily accepted by the congregation. I followed the principle of change by evolution rather than by revolution.

As the congregation became large, the number of decisions requiring action grew significantly. This large counsel approach became too cumbersome. I needed assistance in the administration of the growing staff, programs and ministries. Thus Pastor Dennis Pederson was called in 1979 to serve as managing director and to restructure the organization and to write a new constitution and bylaws. He had the ability to study the situation, seek guidance in prayer, and get revelation on how to implement the solution. Four departments were established: Pastoral Care and Worship; Discipleship, Teaching, and Fellowship; Development, Finance, Business, and Administration; and Evangelism, Renewal, and Missions.

A fifth department, Music, Worship, and Drama, was added later. All staff members and ministries were in one of these departments. A lay board worked alongside of the staff director for each department, and thus providing greater congregational involvement.

During these ten years of explosive growth—1972 to 1981—membership increased from 1,275 to 3,205, a 151 percent growth. Worship service attendance climbed from 402 to 1,773, a 341 percent increase. Income soared from $79,000 to $1,004,000, a jump of 1,271 percent.

Facilities Expansion, and a Second Campus

The rapid growth led to greatly overcrowded facilities. In 1975 the sanctuary was enlarged by adding wings on two sides, thereby doubling its previous size, and by adding a large fellowship hall and a new senior pastor's office. But even with the rental of the North Heights Elementary School on Sunday mornings and Wednesday evenings, all the facilities were soon full and overflowing. Seven services were held in three locations. A Sunday evening prayer and praise Service led by Dick Denny drew many from other churches who sought charismatic teaching and worship. Special recognition needs to be given to Walt Raleigh who led this and previous building programs.

Due to the crowded conditions and the inability to expand further at the Roseville site, the church bought a 46-acre property in Arden Hills for a second campus in 1980. To alleviate the pressure at the Roseville campus and to prepare for expansion into the Arden Hills area, a Sunday morning worship service and Sunday school session were conducted at nearby Irondale High School in New Brighton for one year.

In 1981 the Roseville Area School District closed the North Heights Elementary School and put the building up for sale. The school is directly adjacent to the church's Roseville facilities. The council wrestled with whether or not the church should purchase it. Some expressed that we should "bite the bullet" and build as soon as possible at the Arden Hills site. They felt that at the completion of construction we should close down and sell our Roseville property and relocate our full ministry to the new site.

I believed, as did some other council members, that it would take several years to design and build the new facilities and to raise the funds. In the meantime if the school, which we had been renting for several years, was purchased by outside developers, we would lose the use of the school building for our Sunday morning and Wednesday evening activities.

I also felt we needed to grow much larger in order to be able to build and fund a large enough sanctuary and classroom building to meet the needs of our growing ministry. If we purchased the school building, this would allow for such growth during the next few years. Furthermore, I shared that if we moved out of the Roseville location, we would leave a big hole in the area in that there were only two other Lutheran churches within a two-mile radius. My vision was for North Heights to be one congregation with one staff, one program, and one budget at two locations.

The council operated with a policy requiring unanimous approval for all major decisions. Over a period of several meetings the council had been unable to reach unanimity on which direction to take. A decision needed to be made one way or another regarding the school building or else it would likely be purchased by another buyer. Other interested parties were waiting on our decision. If we wanted the school, they indicated they would withdraw. Since the council was at an impasse, Frank Clawson, the chairman, turned to me and said, "Pastor, it's your decision."

The understanding had always been that in case a decision needed to be made but there was not agreement, the council would defer to the senior pastor to decide. This was the only time that this policy was applied. I had prayed much about direction for the church and together with Dennis Pederson had explored all other possibilities. Every door we examined was not a good fit. We sensed that the Lord had left the door to the school open for North Heights, and that this was the direction to take.

I answered without hesitation, "We will buy the school building." The matter was settled. The school board preferred not to sell it to us, because we had talked about opening our own school. But since there were no other bidders, they agreed to sell it to us for $1,250,000 on a contract for deed with the provision that if we started a school, we would be charged the highest going interest rate for the full duration of the contract. Mortgage rates were at an all-time high at above 20 percent. This delayed the start of our North Heights Christian Academy until we had paid off the contract for deed.

We named the school building the "Community Center" with the vision that it would continue to serve the community as it had been doing since 1895. We had thought of renting out a good portion of the space, but within three years all the space was completely filled with our programs and ministries.

Overcrowding, a persistent challenge most of our history, led to a capital stewardship drive, "Lift Up Your Eyes," in 1984 with John Haney as chairman for construction of worship and education facilities at our Arden Hills site. Three million dollars was raised for the $6.5 million project. The remainder, including the remaining school building debt, was financed through the sale of church bonds. Construction was completed in 1986, and thus was launched a pioneer approach to church programming: one congregation with a common staff, program, budget, and board conducting its ministry on two campuses. This visionary venture of faith has worked surprisingly well. Now two communities receive the full scope of ministries from a mega-church.

Another Merger Issue

Five month after completion of the Arden Hills worship center in 1986 we had to deal with the church merger issue again. Three Lutheran bodies, including our own, were forming the Evangelical Lutheran Church in America (ELCA). North Heights' members were agreed in their opposition to the liberal trends taking place in church and society and to the shift away from the authority of Scripture. But we differed in what direction to take, whether to remain and stand for truth or to leave. Some felt strongly that they could not be members of a denomination which they felt endorsed immoral and unbiblical trends. Others believed that the Lord was calling us to stay in to be a light and prophetic voice, even as did the Old Testament prophets during spiritual and moral apostasy in Israel and Judah. I favored the latter approach.

After much prayer and discussion, the pastoral staff and council joined me in recommending that the church be part of the ELCA. The vote in our congregation was close, 60 percent to 40 percent in favor of joining the merger. The congregational meeting where the issues were discussed and the decision made was the most difficult and contentious in my pastorate. So North Heights became a member congregation in the ELCA.

After this vote, in May 1987, a number of members and active non-members left North Heights. This was a heart-wrenching time. On both sides we sought God's will and desired to be faithful to our conscience, but it was painful.

The financial situation soon reached a serious status due to an increased debt load of $5.5 million, additional expenses with two campuses, departure of members over merger, and a national recession. While our faith was greatly challenged, we found the Lord sufficient to meet our needs. Departmental budgets were reduced, but no staff or programs were cut. That in itself was a miracle.

An Organized Approach to Evangelism

In the 1950s and early 1960s the pastors and parish workers canvassed the area and were instrumental in bringing many to the church and to faith in Christ. During my father's six years as visitation pastor he went to the homes of those without a church connection and to all new residents in our geographic area to invite them to church and to share Jesus. He was successful in bringing many new members into the church and instructing them on the way of salvation. But in these early years apart from the above efforts there was no organized evangelism staff, committee, or program.

In 1972 after the completion of the pastorates of my father and Rev. Rogen and with no immediate replacement in sight, I turned membership over to the Lord. He was to be in charge of bringing into membership those whom He chose to be part of our congregation, and that they take the initiative in joining. I had felt from the beginning of my ministry at North Heights that everyone joining our church needed to know Jesus as their Lord and Savior. We asked each one their faith story. If they were not clear about salvation, I would share the salvation story and give them an opportunity to commit their lives to Christ. As far as I know, all who joined made personal confession of faith in Christ. I placed a spiritual guard over the membership so that the enemy could not get in to work havoc.

Since the renewal of the congregation in 1972, evangelism and growth happened quite spontaneously. People discovered North Heights through a variety of means, and many came to faith or assurance of salvation and experienced the filling with the Holy Spirit at our church. They enthusiastically invited family and friends who came and in turn shared their new-found joy with others. Thus, through natural networking the church exploded in growth. This led to packed out conditions which discouraged overt evangelism efforts by the congregation.

When I discovered in 1973 that people in the new members class were coming from other area churches to join North Heights, I told them I couldn't accept them until I talked with their pastor. The majority came from the same church, and I knew this particular pastor from college. I told him what was taking place, and he gave his approval for us to receive them.

The same thing happened at the next new members' class. Again I went to that same pastor, and again he gave his consent. I did not want to be known by other pastors as a "sheep stealer," nor did I want pastors to complain to my bishop. So I took the initiative of telling him myself of what was transpiring. He said, "I can see the place for a church in the metropolitan area with a charismatic emphasis, and that those drawn to that approach would want to join that church." He gave his endorsement to receiving members from other churches. And in the years that followed they came by the hundreds and thousands.

But by the late 1980s, when we had a new 1,500 seat sanctuary at our second site, we found that it did not fill up just by word of mouth. Some council members felt we should conduct only an 8 O'clock service at Roseville and with the rest to be held at Arden Hills. I expressed the need for viable ministries and programs at both sites. We chose to continue five Sunday morning services at the Roseville worship center and to begin two at the Arden Hills campus. And we conducted two Sunday schools and adult classes at each site. People were free to select whichever location they wished for services and classes. It divided 50/50 as I had expected.

We were also faced with a challenge we had not had to deal with in the past. Formerly, our worship services had been full from the first Sunday after enlargement or expansion. We just became more crowded until new construction could take place, but this was always delayed because we grew faster than we had funds for expansion. Now we were faced with the task of reaching out intentionally to bring more souls into the Kingdom.

A more organized evangelism effort ensued. Evangelism staff and programs were instituted to reach those who had no church home and those who did not know Christ as Savior and Lord. Muriel Jensen became the staff champion for evangelistic outreach. Every week there were people who came to saving faith and new life in Christ as well as those who were healed, filled with the Spirit and who experienced answered prayer. At every service people came forward seeking prayer for a variety of needs. Praying for people was a staple of our church, not only at worship services but at all activities and at any time. We expected miracles and witnessed many through the years. Over time attendance at Arden Hills increased, while it declined at Roseville.)

Major ministries were birthed

Greg Olson expressed the faith atmosphere of our church well. At a staff meeting in the mid 1970s he described North Heights as a seedbed where visions are planted, and they grow and flourish.

That is fitting, for the language of the Holy Spirit is "visions, dreams and prophesy," we note from Joel 2 and Acts 2:

> *And in the last days it shall be, God declares,*
> *That I will pour out my Spirit upon all flesh,*
> *And your sons and your daughters shall prophesy,*
> *And your young men shall see visions,*
> *And your old men shall dream dreams;*
> *Yea, and on my menservants and my maidservants*
> *in those days,*
> *I will pour out my Spirit; and they shall prophesy.*

We sought an environment where people were free to dream, see visions and speak forth the word the Lord laid on their heart. As a result many such Spirit-birthed visions became reality. A few of these are noted here.

A television ministry was birthed in the mid 1980s and continued for three years under the name *The North Heights Hour*, and later incorporated as *Renewal International*. It began in an interview format and later was changed to telecasting our worship services. Our program appeared on twelve stations in ten states and by cable in parts of Canada and by satellite over Western Europe. Our vision was to reach those not attending church with the good news of Jesus Christ so they may receive Him as Lord and Savior and to expose church members to spiritual renewal so they may seek new life for their church.

Church On Fire

With the opening of the *North Heights Christian Academy* in 1988, a dream of long standing became reality. Dr. Victoria Jacobson was the original designer of the curriculum and was the initial principal and administrator. Jeff Taylor has been the principal since 1997. Today 260 students are enrolled and receiving education from a Christian perspective in grades K-8. The peak enrollment was 279 in the 2002-03 school year, which is maximum capacity. A high school has been envisioned, but there are not ample facilities to accommodate it. Most of our graduates enroll at nearby Concordia Academy.

In 1989 Rev. Thom and Jan Hardwick were called to serve as *Minister and Coordinator of Music and Drama*. They began performances of *The Splendor of Christmas* and *The Passion Play*. These outstanding productions had a major impact within the church, and they became the largest outreach ministry of the church, together with the Freedom Celebration on the Fourth of July weekend. Four hundred fifty volunteers from the church served as cast members with several hundred others participating behind the scenes. The re-enactment of the life of Christ had a powerful effect on the cast members as well as on the audience.

Every performance was sold out as soon as tickets went on sale. More than a half million people attended these productions. Through video tapes and television presentations of the musical dramas, multitudes more were exposed to the Good News of Jesus Christ. Portions of both productions were aired on national television throughout India to 400 million viewers. Christmas, Palm Sunday, Easter, and Independence weekend services feature special music and drama performances attracting thousands.

Our members caught the vision of sharing Jesus Christ as Lord and Savior and of spreading the gospel and spiritual renewal worldwide. Pastor Bob Cottingham initiated a *Mission's Outreach Program* in 1982, when he served on the staff of the church and the Lay Ministry Training Center. Since then scores of members have served as missionaries and hundreds have gone out on short-term mission trips. Dr. Dennis Pederson and John Haney sparked strong response to Mission Russia, a major evangelism endeavor in many Russian cities along the Volga River. Dr. Allen Swanson, called in 1995 as Missions and Evangelism Pastor, significantly increased our vision for and involvement in local and global cross-cultural outreach. Some forty families and individuals are currently serving as missionaries from our church.

The congregation has approached these opportunities in a positive manner. In 1995 we launched a ministry expansion fund drive, *"Catch the Vision,"* for building a Family Life Center on our Arden hills campus. The need was urgent. Sunday school classes had to meet in hallways because there was not sufficient space. Those leaving the worship service while it was still in progress, might have to step over or around children as a class had no other place to meet than in the doorway. To alleviate the over crowded facilities modular units were placed at both campuses. But this did not resolve the problem. It simply allowed more to come to classes or services.

The construction of the very large Family Life Center allowed for outreach to many more families who need Jesus as Savior and Lord. This ministry center was constructed during the fiftieth anniversary year as a thanksgiving offering to the Lord for His past abundant blessings and as a mission offering for the purpose of reaching those who had not heard and did not know Jesus personally as Redeemer. Even with this addition we still had a space problem.

Church On Fire

We believe that both spiritual and numerical growths are biblical. From 1982 to 1996 membership jumped from 3,205 to 6,568, a 105 percent growth. Attendance grew from 1, 773 to 3,304, or 90 percent. And the church's income increased from $1,004,000 to $6,462,000, a 544% gain.

Burden for Revival
Chapter 13

O Lord, I have heard of what you have done,
and I am filled with awe.
Now do again in our times
the great deed you used to do.
Be merciful even when you are angry.
Habakkuk 3:2 TEV

From the beginning there have been those who have had a
burden and vision for revival, first in their own lives and families
and then in the church and community. We have prayed
individually and in small groups for the Spirit to stir spiritual
awakening in our hearts and in the lives of many others. The Lord
has been gracious and has answered our prayers. We have been
enriched by continuous renewal the past decades. But we are
reminded that every generation needs its own revival and not
simply to draw from the previous renewal or from awakenings of
previous ages. In effect, in each season of the church's life people
are called to be instruments for spiritual awakening, and this
through fervent prayer, Spirit-empowerment proclamation and
holy living. So we are challenged to continue to prayer for fresh
visitations of the Spirit.

For instance, in the 1960s a group of men met each Monday
evening at the altar to pray for revival, and as a result over time
the congregation experienced spiritual awakening. In the 1970s a
dozen persons met weekly to pray for renewal of the whole
church and to foster spiritual awakening. This group took the
name *Concerned Christians for Spiritual Renewal*. They witnessed
answer to their prayers.

Under Leonard Ohlsson's leadership this group prayed the faith budget into reality. They started a book ministry in 1973 called *Maranatha Bookstore* under Lorna Rogers' direction, and she and the bookstore are still serving the church and community thirty-five years later. This prayer group initiated a renewal section in the church's weekly newsletter, *North Heights Hi-Lights*. Fern Leben's wrote these inspiring articles so as to foster personal spiritual renewal, and these continued for several years. This group also published *A Call To Renewal*, a quarterly magazine which was sent to every Lutheran church in the nation with the goal of sparking a vision for spiritual awakening in the hearts of pastors and laity. Bill and Roberta Dahlke gave leadership to this publication.

Several families, many of them from the above renewal prayer group, went to San Antonio for *"Expo 73"* conducted by *Campus Crusade for Christ*, a powerful evangelistic ministry under the visionary leadership of Dr. Bill Bright. The North Heights group returned home with a vision for evangelizing our inactive members and reaching out into the community. Jim Lebens had the vision for this home visitation evangelistic outreach. Every week teams went out presenting the gospel using *The Four Spiritual Laws* booklet.

A *Special Education* ministry for mentally challenged teens and adults was initiated by Louise Harris, who gave able leadership to this program until her death. Dr. John Rynders, a noted professor at the University of Minnesota in this field, helped birth this program and has given guidance and support to this ministry. More than one hundred attend classes and services Sunday mornings at both campuses. An extension of this outreach is the *"I Am His"* club which provides spiritual and social programs on Tuesday evenings. Jesus' love and compassion for each one is shared in a beautiful way and it is heart-warming to see their response of love for Jesus.

Institutes on Church Renewal were conducted regularly for a decade. Scores of pastors and church leaders attended from across the nation and around the world. The purpose was to inspire vision for spiritual awakening, to share principles for parish renewal, to pray for individual and congregational needs, and to provide networks of encouragement and prayer. These institutes gave impetus to the formation of Lutheran renewal committees in several countries, mainly in northern Europe. Dr. Jerry Lalla gave administrative leadership to the Institutes.

Training Lay People for Ministry

During the peak of the Charismatic Renewal Movement I felt the need for a Bible school with a Lutheran charismatic emphasis. There were some young people who wanted to do short-term or longer-term cross-cultural ministry or mission work, and they needed training. Others sought healing in their lives, while others desired a stronger biblical foundation to their faith. These were motivating factors for founding a Bible school.

In 1981 our congregation engaged Dr. Byron Schmid to develop such a school. He was a pastor and former staff personnel with the Lutheran Council USA and with The American Lutheran Church.

The design for the new school incorporated four major components: 1) classroom instruction for establishing biblical and doctrinal foundation; 2) individual and group discipleship for faith formation and accountability; 3) group prayer and worship for growth in spirituality; and 4) practical ministry training and outreach involvement.

In 1982 the *Lay Ministry Training Center International* (LMTC) began operation as a two-year Bible school and training center to equip lay persons for full-time ministry and for lay ministry in one's church. It served our congregation, but even more so the larger charismatic renewal both nationally and internationally. The school sought a balance between Word and Spirit. During the school's twenty-three year existence, Dr. Schmid, Don Fladland, and David Jore served successively as presidents. Each year 30 to 35 resource or adjunct faculty taught courses.

Over five hundred students from 33 foreign nations and 28 states attended LMTC. In its later years a number of students came from Eastern Europe, and they are currently serving in a variety of ministries in their own countries.

More than one hundred graduates have gone into full-time ministry or are in further ministry training. Some started Bible schools in other countries. Until its closing in 2005, this small training center made a significant impact far beyond its size.

Ministries Birthed at North Heights

Various ministries were birthed at North Heights and became affiliated ministries of the church. These include the following.

Intercollegiate Fellowship Renewal (ICFR) was a Spirit-filled ministry to college students on campuses in the region, principally at Lutheran colleges. The acronym ICFR (I See Afar) expressed the large vision of its founder and leader Greg Olson. It was to expose students to the outpouring of the Holy Spirit so that they might experience the powerful transformation the Spirit brings. Fellowship groups were developed on seven college campuses. Periodic retreats drew hundreds of students for powerful weekends of worship, teaching, and ministry. The fruit of this Spirit-filled ministry is seen in the large numbers who indicated that the ICFR ministry transformed their lives during a crucial decision-making time.

Eagles' Wings Ministries, an outreach to homosexuals, their families and those afflicted with AIDS for transformation in Christ, was founded in 1988 by North Heights members Rev. Wendell and Nancy Anderson and Dottie Ludwig. Its mission was to inform concerned persons and churches about the origins and effects of homosexuality and to assist those seeking freedom from the homosexual life. This was the only transformation ministry in the ELCA. Its staff members were invited to present the transformation perspective to the ELCA Council of Bishops, the ELCA Church Council, synod assemblies, churches, and other forums. Their compassionate witness was heard even if not always accepted by all.

Praise of His Glory, a prayer and retreat ministry, was a vision given by the Lord to Joan Nesser, and it was birthed in 1976. It was housed at North Heights until 1990, when it built the Christos prayer retreat center in Centerville. Prayer retreats are held regularly at the center.

In 1972, *Love Lines Telephone Counseling Ministry* under the leadership of Dan and Diane Morstad began 24-hour Christian phone counseling. In the thirty-six years since, the counseling service has received over two million calls, of which 31,000 received salvation. In addition, Love Lines has assisted in starting 115 Christian telephone counseling centers in 28 countries.

Church On Fire

In 1977, Dr. Jerry Lalla began the *School of Health and Healing*. Weekly teaching seminars are held at the church in which various topics dealing with physical, spiritual and emotional health and healing are addressed. A weekly TV teaching program aired on local cable channels.

Although not birthed by North Heights, a significant ministry that born at the Roseville sanctuary altar was *Minnesota Family Council*. On a Wednesday evening in the spring of 1983 I went to receive prayer and communion from Wendell and Roberta Brown. Wendell was an elder in our church and Roberta was state director for the Legislative Prayer Chain. The State Legislature was in session at the time. We were each concerned about major social issues before this legislative body. A coalition representing more liberal churches was the only visible voice speaking for the religious community. In many issues we were at odds with their perspective. After prayer seeking divine guidance we felt led to call together religious leaders and laity who shared similar concerns and convictions. Two gatherings were held in our dining room. *The Berean League* was formed to guide churches and the public and to influence legislators concerning social and political issues under consideration. The name was later changed to the *Minnesota Family Council* and the ministry expanded significantly. It plays an important role in the values battle in our state.

Fostering Renewal Worldwide

North Heights has been involved in a significant way with various Lutheran Renewal Service Organizations for the purpose of fostering spiritual awakening and of serving those involved in charismatic renewal. These organizations included *Lutheran Charismatic Renewal Services* under Larry Christenson's leadership, the International Lutheran Center for Church Renewal and the publication *Lutheran Renewal International* under Dr. Dennis Pederson's leadership, and currently the *International Lutheran Renewal Center,* identified simply as *Lutheran Renewal,* directed formerly by Larry Christenson and now by Paul Anderson. The offices of each of these ministries were housed at North Heights. These were coordinating organizations for charismatic renewal among Lutherans.

Rev. Norris Wogan had a vision for a Lutheran charismatic conference. He shared this with a few of us, and out of this was birthed the first *International Lutheran Conference on the Holy Spirit* (ILCOHS) held in August 1972 in the Minneapolis Auditorium. Ten to twelve thousand attended this exciting gathering. It hit the front page of local newspapers and received national publicity. This was among the first large public exposures to charismatic renewal and spiritual gifts in mainline Protestant denominations. It had been growing quietly in home groups and in a few churches across the country for the previous decade.

The power of God was manifest mightily. Large numbers committed their lives to Christ, were filled with the Holy Spirit, and were healed. The worship was vibrant. The atmosphere was electrifying. The messages fanned into flame the fire of the Holy Spirit in a multitude of hearts. The surprising thing was that this phenomenon took place among Lutherans who were often viewed as stodgy and unemotional. Charismatic renewal had now come out into the open and become an internationally recognized dynamic movement. This took place just a few blocks from the national headquarters of our denomination.

This conference became an annual event which attracted as many as 25,000 in 1976 when Léon Joseph Cardinal Suenens of Belgium spoke. From its inception the conference was ecumenical. North

Heights' staff and members were vitally involved in many organizational and ministry aspects of the conferences. Dick Denny was the able business manager for twenty years. I served as chairman from 1972 to 1995, the last several years as co-chair with Larry Christenson, the director of the International Lutheran Renewal Center. Dennis Pederson assisted me in operations.

In 1977 the Lutheran Conference was held in Kansas City in conjunction with the *Conference on Charismatic Renewal in the Christian Church* attended by 50,000. In 1987 our conference joined in the same configuration at New Orleans Super Dome where again 50,000 were gathered.

The decades of the 1970s and 1980s were the peak of attendance at Charismatic Renewal conferences, and maybe the height of the movement. The influence of the renewal reached beyond anyone's ability to measure. I believe we can rightly say that the Charismatic/Pentecostal movement has been the largest and most far-reaching revival in history. While there has been rampant decline among mainline denominations in Europe and North America, churches in the Southern Hemisphere have been burgeoning. Church statisticians estimate that as many as 800 million Christians in the world are participants in this mighty move of the Spirit, or can be classified as charismatic/Pentecostal, and the bulk of them are in Africa, Asia and Latin America.

We are privileged by God's grace to be part of such a move, which possibly could be the vast end-time ingathering of souls into the kingdom. Yet, multitudes still have not heard the good news of salvation and new life in Christ. Nor have they seen the demonstration of the Spirit's mighty power to deliver from Satan's kingdom of darkness and entrance into Christ's kingdom of light. These significant challenges call for our complete surrender to the Lord and our full empowerment with the Holy Spirit.

Church On Fire

Passing the Baton
Chapter 14

According to the grace of God given to me,
like a skilled master builder I laid a foundation,
and another man is building upon it.
Let each man take care how he builds upon it.
(1 Corinthians 3:10)

When should I lay down my ministry at North Heights? This was a question I asked the Lord as I was drawing near to the age of 65, and especially after I had passed that milestone.

Some years earlier the Council of Elders had encouraged me to search for a likely candidate who could be groomed to succeed me. My efforts failed to lead me to a possible successor.

"Lord, I Give Up!

In 1996 I was invited to speak at a renewal conference in Papua New Guinea. On my return home I suffered jet lag. Being unable to sleep I decided to make it an all-night prayer time. Some crucial issues loomed before me. A major one had to do with when to retire from North Heights. I was 67 at the time. How long should I continue serving? On the one hand, I did not want to overstay my effectiveness. I wanted to step down while the church was still growing and moving forward and not when it was starting to decline. Yet on the other hand, I still had energy and vision for the task. North Heights was such an integral part of my life and identity that I had great difficulty seeing myself separated from her. I sought the Lord's will and timing, but no clear word came. Was I willing to let go? That was the issue.

That night after hours of intense internal struggle, I finally surrendered the church and the decision to the Lord. I said, "Lord, I give up! I quit! I will resign immediately." I wrote a letter of resignation, then woke Bonnie up and read it to her, and I went to bed and slept peacefully. The next day I waited for the Spirit to confirm this decision with my spirit. What came to me was that I should not to act on it yet.

The next night I still could not sleep, so again I had an all-night prayer wrestling match with the Lord. This time He dealt with me on an issue even more personal and painful. This too became an extended struggle. Was I willing to yield to the will of the Lord? I knew that if I did not surrender the matter to the Lord, I would not advance any further in my Christian life. This is a principle in the Christian life—failure to yield to and obey the Lord will be a roadblock to further growth, and in fact will lead to decline in one's relationship with the Lord.

After an extended struggle I recognized that I had no other choice but to surrender to the Lord. I was reminded of Jacob's decisive all-night wrestling with the Lord at Jabbok (Genesis 32:24). Finally, I placed the matter on the altar. I laid down my life completely before the Lord in brokenness. The heavy burdened was then lifted from me.

Now the Lord could reveal his plan to me. He showed me the image of a relay race, indicating that the conclusion of my ministry at North Heights and the transfer of leadership to a new senior pastor should be like the passing of the baton to the next runner. In other racing events the qualified persons run the prescribed distance, and the race ends. Then preparations are made for the next race to be run. The lag time between races could be quite lengthy. North Heights would lose its momentum if there were to be an interim period before the next pastor came on board. In the relay race model there would be a seamless transfer of leadership.

Furthermore, the direction I received was for a three-year transition process in which the congregation would clarify its identity, or its DNA, and identify the qualities to seek in the new senior pastor. Candidates would be interviewed and selection made. The process would be bathed in prayer, and the Lord's guidance would be sought.

At the next council of elders meeting I announced my retirement and shared the three-year transition process as a recommendation. I indicated that in this scenario I would continue at full speed while my successor was being sought. When the selection had been made, he would be brought on board during the last phase of my run so that he could gain speed. Then, as we were running side-by-side, both at full speed, I would pass the baton to him, and would fade away while he continued the race. The council accepted this proposal.

God Prepares My Successor

The search process led to the selection of Pastor Robert Cottingham. He had been a convert during my early years at North Heights. He, his wife Sandi, and their two children, Chris and Robin, had moved from Austin, Minnesota, to their new home one mile north of the Roseville church in 1968. They attended North Heights and found what they had been thirsting for, the abundant life that Jesus offers. It was my father who led Bob to faith in Christ. They were part of a growing number of younger families on fire for the Lord. Along with several other families, they adopted a Korean orphan, Paul. Bonnie and I became sponsors for Paul in baptism.

Evangelist Herbert Mjorud prayed with Bob Cottingham for the baptism with the Holy Spirit and prophesied over him that he was to go into the ministry. After attending Augsburg College and graduating from Luther Seminary, he and his wife Sandi served as missionaries in Africa. Then in 1982 he served on our staff and that of the Lay Ministry Training Center, after which he was called to be Africa director for Lutheran World Relief.

In 1987 he received a call to serve as pastor at Lutheran Church of the Master in Brooklyn Center, a northern suburb of Minneapolis. In 1999 North Heights extended him a call to serve as its new senior pastor.

The Baton Is Passed

The "passing of the baton" services were held at the five Roseville services on September 26, 1999 and at the two Arden Hills services on October 3, 1999. Many events took place during the preceding weeks in which we honored the pioneers and leaders who served and sacrificed to make the church a dynamic force in the kingdom of God. The members honored Bonnie and me together with our family in several spectacular ways. We were deeply moved by their expression of affection and appreciation. Our words are inadequate in expressing our love for the North Heights body of believers.

Now nine years later, the congregation remains large and strong. People are being brought into the Kingdom on a consistent basis and are growing spiritually. The church continues to reach out to the community and nations with the love of Christ and the good news of a personal relationship with God through Christ. The Holy Spirit's power and gifts are manifestly present in the life of the congregation.

As of this writing, in the summer of 2008, I am beginning my fourth interim pastorate since stepping down from North Heights, and this is at Lutheran Church of the Master where Bob Cottingham had previously served. In addition I am writing, speaking, and serving as president of *Renewal International,* a ministry which supports mission work in Madagascar and mentors other ministries.

A Continuing Burden for Revival

I confess that by no means have I arrived. I need to be renewed on a continuous basis. And this is true for every believer. Jeremiah has expressed it well in his Lamentations:

The steadfast love of the LORD never ceases,
his mercies never come to an end;
they are new every morning;
great is thy faithfulness. (3:22-23)

Oh, that our hearts would cry out for the Lord to pour out His Spirit anew and afresh on us and on our churches to revive us so that we may be the Church on Fire!

This God-given plea for spiritual revitalization remains with me and stirs my heart. It is a vision for daily renewal and continuous revival in my life and that of individuals, families, churches, denominations, and nations. I have a special burden for spiritual awakening in the Lutheran Church. My heart cry is, *Lord, revive your church beginning with me.*

How does this take place? The Apostle Paul expressed it well in 2 Corinthians 3:18:

> And we all with unveiled face, beholding the glory of the Lord, are being changed into his likeness from one degree of glory to another, for this comes from the Lord who is the Spirit.

Some translations read *reflecting the glory of the Lord* instead of *beholding*. It is both/and, for as we behold the glory of the Lord we will reflect it. This is revival life, an ongoing renewing in our spirit with the Lord's glory. As we seek the face of the Lord, the Spirit is transforming us into His image and concurrently reflects His image through us.

May our desire be that as expressed by Paul in
Philippians 3:7-8a, 10:

> But whatever gain I had, I counted as loss for the sake of Christ. Indeed I count everything as loss because of the surpassing worth of knowing Christ Jesus my Lord...that I may know him and the power of his resurrection, and may share his sufferings, becoming like him in his death.

Oh, that our heart's desire would be to know the Lord Jesus Christ more fully and intimately! Invite the Spirit to remove everything that clutters your life and hinders you from giving your wholehearted attention to the Lord! Implore the Spirit to open the eyes of your heart and to reveal to your inner being the glory of the Lord!